BOOK OF
ARAUCARIA
CROSSWORDS
VOLUME 3

'Araucaria is the most infuriatingly ingenious setter working today. Even if, like me, you seldom complete his crosswords, there's a masochistic pleasure to be had from going through his solutions, spotting all those moments where he pulled the carpet out from under you.'
Ian Rankin

'Araucaria is quite simply the master compiler of his generation.'
Hugh Stephenson, crossword editor of The Guardian

'They say that doing crosswords extends your mental life and helps ward off senility. In which case, most Araucaria fans can expect to become centenarians.'
Simon Hoggart

'Discovering Araucaria was like falling in love.'
Sandy Balfour

'An Araucaria any day of the week is one of the world's great treats, while an Araucaria on Saturday, rhyming jigsaw or otherwise, is the ultimate justification for the invention of Saturdays.'
David McKie

'Araucaria's wit, warmth, erudition and mischief never fail to lighten our (late) breakfast table. We always want to say thank you, loudly and publicly. And now we have.'
Alan Plater

'My constant bedtime companion ... '
Prunella Scales

'I have known John Graham since I was 13, but I had corresponded with him for two or three years before, even at that age having been hooked on crosswords. He had become my idol when I saw one of his famous 'theme' puzzles in *The Guardian*. Now, almost 30 years later, the ever-popular Guardian of the Monkey Puzzle Tree is here again with another cruciverbal tour de force.'
John Henderson, Enigmatist of The Guardian.

CHAMBERS

BOOK OF
ARAUCARIA
CROSSWORDS
VOLUME 3

CHAMBERS

CHAMBERS
An imprint of Chambers Harrap Publishers Ltd
7 Hopetoun Crescent
Edinburgh
EH7 4AY

www.chambers.co.uk

First published by Chambers Harrap Publishers Ltd 2006

A CIP catalogue record for this book is available from the British Library.

ISBN-13: 978 0550 10196 9
ISBN-10: 0550 10196 9

Chambers Editor: Hazel Norris
Crossword Proof Checkers: Ross Beresford and Christine Jones
Prepress Controller: Heather Macpherson
Prepress Manager: Clair Simpson
Publishing Manager: Patrick White

Designed and typeset by Chambers Harrap Publishers Ltd, Edinburgh
Printed by CPI Group (UK) Ltd, Croydon, CR0 4YY

FOREWORD
by Simon Hoggart

As a *Guardian* writer I'm obviously biased, but I very much like the way our cryptic crosswords have by-lines so you know who compiled them. This matters, because you need to be mentally prepared, as you would be meeting any other old friend. *The Times* doesn't do this, presumably because of some ancient and immutable tradition. Perhaps the *Times* crossword editor would like to go back to the days when even articles didn't have names on top. 'President Caught In Bed With Goat. By A Correspondent.'

But *The Guardian* does tell you, and there is a special delight in the morning at finding a well-loved name at the bottom of the inside back page. We all have our favourites: mine are Bunthorne, Shed, Paul and, these days, Brummie. The others are first-rate too, but there is an extra frisson of pleasure in seeing a *nom de plume* that means your trip into work will be less dreary, that your morning coffee will give you an extra lift or that you can nag away at 24 across during a particularly dull meeting. I work at the House of Commons, and it is my boast that I once got all but two lights in a Paul puzzle while taking a perfectly adequate note of the Select Committee on Public Administration.

The doyen of all *Guardian* setters is, of course, John Graham, or Araucaria. John is 85 years old, a retired vicar, lives in a village close to Huntingdon and usually has many crosswords on the go, returning to each from time to time, like a chess grandmaster playing several boards at once. John is not only liked but loved by solvers. I've been present a couple of times when he has spoken to fans, once at *The Guardian*, once at the Hay-on-Wye festival, and each time someone got up to thank him for all the pleasure he had brought over the years, and the rest of the audience cheered.

Why is he so popular? It is, I suspect, the sheer wit of his clueing, and its brevity. No word is ever redundant or out of place. Even when you're being fooled, it's done by such cunning sleight of hand that you don't mind. Some Ximenean purists claim that he breaks the rules, and so he does – but never in a way that defrauds us. There can be almost as much pleasure in learning an unsolved light next morning as in getting it on the day.

Then there is the dazzling inventiveness of his crosswords – and the book you hold in your hand contains 60 examples of that. John invented the alphabetical jigsaw crossword, in which lights are written in wherever they will fit. It is typical of him that the perimeter puzzles – there are many in this book – are made slightly easier by having the clues listed in alphabetical order of the answers.

How does he compile the puzzles? Out of his own head, obviously, though he did let slip at Hay that he uses *Chambers Words for Crosswords and Wordgames*, and now intends to use the Chambers website to help fill in grids. (You can get help with your solutions in the same place, by going to www.chambers.co.uk, then hitting 'Word Wizards'.) He also uses a set of Scrabble® tiles, which I suppose is how he came by what is probably his most famous clue: 'Poetical scene with surprisingly chaste Lord Archer vegetating (3,3,8,12)', which leads to THE OLD VICARAGE, GRANTCHESTER, which just happens to be both a poetical site and Jeffrey Archer's home.

We all have our favourite Araucaria moments – beside a roaring fire on a cold winter evening, or happily filling in time on a long and otherwise tiresome plane journey. Sitting in the garden on a warm summer's day, a glass of beer to hand and a virgin Araucaria on one's lap may not be everyone's idea of total bliss, but it will certainly do me for now.

Simon Hoggart
March 2006

INTRODUCTION

Literature and crosswords might be thought uneasy bedfellows. I fear that anyone who has been truly bitten by the crossword bug is severely handicapped in the appreciation of literature. Once upon a time – it was a long time ago so I remember it well – I fell in love with 'Ode to a Nightingale', and was especially smitten where, after the fantastic 'viewless wings of poesy' stanza, comes that line of monosyllabic simplicity – 'I cannot see what flowers are at my feet'. When I think of that line now, I see that it has four sections of seven letters each which would make a nice perimetrical jigsaw (examples within if you don't know this animal), leaving FEET to be fitted in somewhere, and then I'm away, trying to see where my FEET will go. But where now are the shivers that once went down my spine?

Setters are much worse than solvers, of course; I believe it is quite possible to be a regular solver and still have an uncorrupted love for words in other contexts. I have tried not to make matters worse for you in this collection: there are not very many actual quotations (other than those in puzzle 20) and none I hope that are violently sacrilegious; the literariness consists mainly of names – of people, poems, books, etc – though I have allowed myself to poke a little innocent fun at great writers when they seem to invite it, as Wordsworth often does – see for instance puzzle 17. If I manage to amuse you and test your solving skills, good; but I hope also that some of you in the course of solving may turn the pages of some real books and revisit old friends or acquire new ones.

The puzzles are in no particular order; no way of ordering them seemed to make sense, so I have left it to chance, and you can solve them in any order you like. Some puzzles may require some looking-up; but this is a book, and it is assumed you will have time to do this. Apart from a complete Shakespeare (the which if you do not possess, go and buy at once, if necessary instead of this) you should be able to manage, though a dictionary of quotations and an anthology such as the *Oxford Book of English Verse* could help. There is little modern stuff here, partly because my tastes are necessarily those of an octogenarian, but chiefly because 'classical' stuff is usually more accessible and more crossword-friendly. Welcome to 'words that teem with hidden meaning – like Basingstoke': for I do believe that this kind of exercise will help to preserve, if not to 'restore us to, our saner selves'.

Araucaria
March 2006

ACKNOWLEDGEMENTS

This book is the result of a conspiracy between Christine Jones (my more-than-agent), Ross Beresford (my proof checker) and Hazel Norris (my editor at Chambers) to get my shambolic material into some sort of coherent order and make it as fit as it ever could be to lay before potential solvers. Any remaining infelicities are my fault, and if these are few the credit is theirs.

At an earlier stage these puzzles passed through the hands of Antoinette McInnes, the 'Woman in Wiltshire', who has sent them back to me with comments such as 'very hard', 'not anag', 'who he?' – checking my errors and keeping me in touch with the real world.

And for this volume my special thanks to those men and women of genius who have constructed that other world – whether more or less real who shall say? – where Perdita picks her flowers and Pickwick preserves his innocence and prayers are said in proper English – to the Writers of Literature, my deep and eternal gratitude.

Araucaria

ABOUT THE AUTHOR

John Graham began creating crosswords at the age of nine, and his first published crossword puzzle appeared in the *Manchester Guardian* in 1958. He has set for *The Guardian* ever since, taking the pseudonym Araucaria, meaning 'monkey puzzle tree'. He also compiles crosswords for the *Financial Times* as Cinephile, and founded the crossword magazine *1 Across* in 1984. A retired clergyman, he lives in Cambridgeshire. He was awarded the MBE in 2005.

CROSSWORDS

Perimeter: That's so, what's more: Lakeland pass with a middle but no end, and class at school keeping its class symbol, are equal (following appeal to Time by 6) (2,2,3,4,1,4,3,2,2,5).

1   Ventilator of melody by Tennessee Williams character (3-5)
2   Actor makes a record – Bill's first number (2,6)
3   Our man in wherever gives morning drink to a beetle (10)
4   Revealer of star and moon, a royal personage (10)
5   Spanish cloak or article of headgear, with pie for the fully armed (4)
6   Version of 27 I love – I loved 19 and 17 loved me (7)
7   Where Monty's men fought partly to repel a demonstration (2,4)
8   Superior companion for the Queen, that is (4)
9   German girl telling awful lies (4)
10   Flower girl, she wrecked a location of Man (5,3)
11   I get a concession – short time, and long time for termites (8)
12   Work of art inflamed swine with knock on his head (10)
13   Writer of village school stories heard to get book wrong? (7)
14   Capital setter follows aristocrat without bearing (7)
15   Character of Landor's first love (6)
16   Man of theatre sounds like nobody (4)
17   I got involved with Viola (6)
18   'Ave confidence about success with green, maybe serpentine, rock (6)
19   Noble duke and other ranks with the wrong love (6)
20   Capital excessive with Scots not at home (6)
21   Miss Edgeworth's castle has baggage shelf torn (8)
22   Knot could be a great barrier (4)
23   Waterways could be dire (7)
24   Model ruler said to be moderator (8)
25   Place scholar with Jewish comedian to go and sit out (10)
26   Fertile outgrowth achieving verisimilitude (4,2,4)
27   Ruler gets a ruler's part (4)
28   Punter ends badly with some of allocation unused (10)

If 15ac = 9dn with a new ending and part of 24 = 20, then 2 = 8, 9ac = 11, 14 = 12 and 27 = 21dn. The persons concerned are partially clued.

ACROSS

8   Put 2 right into London hospital (9)
9   Enthusiast for US city (5)
10 Get in first if you want to give pet perm (3-4)
11 Wodehouse hero (7)
12 Papal follower in time (5)
14 English heroine (from Somerset) – strike off her place (9)
15 Return of love among rivers (6)
17 Viola's cabin is nearly going to be in red (6)
20 Close to 81 in the table, in ivory (9)
21 Set fire to church on hill (5)
23 Bunting or bit of flag in fashion (7)
24 End of Leviathan, 1000 degree puzzle (7)
26 Major opera? (5)
27 Michael entertaining the Queen (9)

DOWN

1   Processed card that was stolen (6)
2   Sixpence, no tips (4)
3   Environmental protester or politician in government? (6)
4   Relative born – may she perish! (7)
5   Drink tea with errant Liberals (7)
6   Nearly sound asleep, as it were, deafblind legend takes a dive (10)
7   Glen with theatrical associations when morning comes will have playwright (4,4)
9   Take the wrong road in later stage of expedition by car (7)
13 Take cheering introduction, say, with time – long time – for parasitic insects (10)
15 Hunting dog to hold nuke prepared (8)
16 She drowned the sound of Lamb (7)
18 Treatment centres for numbers in the Indian Civil Service (7)
19 Explosive used by machine wrecker with second change (7)
21 Desire, inflamed, rising (6)
22 Drake's end in port (Newbolt) (6)
25 Post protecting body (4)

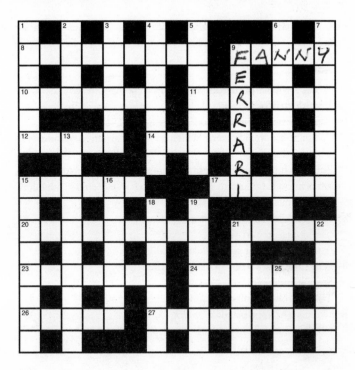

6s of the 4 25 featured its members 18 4, 28 5, 23ac 22 and 20 1dn; their clues are partial.

ACROSS

1 Good guy with petty quarrel refuses to compromise (6,3)
6 It has little weight (5)
9 Ultramarine blue shrub not thus inverted, I see? (7)
10 Father strict on subject of which Johnson admitted ignorance (7)
11 The show must (4)
12 Shrew, last outburst done, is without anger (9)
14 An acknowledgment to Pecksniff's employee seems grudging (2,1,5)
15 Term is over: I'm on strike (6)
18 My first king entertaining me separately (6)
20 Chubby lad at fort (8)
23 Another one held by Scots lord and left (9)
24 Bird saying he's won? (4)
26 Steer some mules into obstruction (7)
27 Thatcher sounds like a saint in the Channel Islands (7)
28 Girl caught in possession of dog (5)
29 Confirm attempt to enter incomplete prophet (9)

DOWN

1 Spaniards up for drug (9)
2 Benign growth from port to (almost) sultanate (7)
3 Hamlet had an easy part (4)
4 Choose evil (unedited) (8)
5 Two males (chasing females) (6)
6 Nothing in Imogen's mate (10)
7 Give it here! (7)
8 Round sounds (5)
13 Not zoology or botany or mainly (for example) metamorphosis (10)
16 Hurry to desert in Mansfield Park (9)
17 —— the centre of the target? Nonsense – spit and polish (8)
19 The Empress got the swag (7)
21 Interim arrangement for London stations? (7)
22 One of a pennyworth maybe pulled out (6)
23 Father of the quadruple bottle, first of which comes in undiluted (5)
25 If you can't beat with it, join it (4)

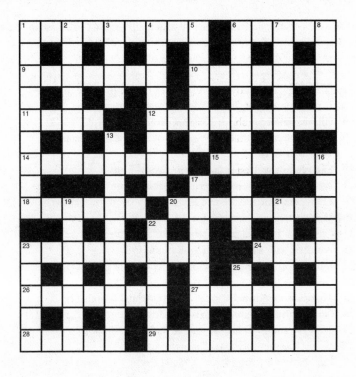

Across clues that end (somewhat misleadingly) with '(7)' contain hidden anagrams of their solutions which are authors of a kind – the only precisely such that I could think of. Other clues are normal.

ACROSS

1   Lydia rapturously clasped Major Forster's hand (7)
5   All was in readiness for Emma's jaunt to Box Hill (7)
9   Some antonyms look like synonyms, eg Jane's 'Sense' and 'Sensibility' (7)
10   Such excess will be disgusting to Fanny (7)
11   Poor Miss Taylor! – with Baby Weston to nurse (7)
13   Catherine Morland we humbly admit to be no proper heroine (7)
14   Vegetarian diet is crazy (4)
15   Cricket or football player strictly for the birds? (10)
18   Number with the German look in joint (10)
20,12   Full name of 28 – or extremely minor Kipling – character (4,5,6)
22   Colonel Brandon was first with the news (7)
23   Mr Collins was the Bennets' hated cousin (7)
26   Sir Thomas brought Fanny a little something from Antigua (7)
27   How long was Mr Elliot's stay at Bath? (7)
28   Elinor thought the colonel amiable enough (7)
29   Pug discovered the admiral's leg which he took for a lamppost (7)

DOWN

1   Hand around academic from Dijon's sermon (5)
2   See 14
3   Report of big house serving good food (5)
4   8 to take to court (3)
5   Expecting a turn-up from the Shrew (Iambic version) (11)
6   Proteus' girl and associates contain complex numbers (5,3)
7   Pussy's voice raised when undergoing confinement? (5,2)
8   Poles cover America with black eyes (5)
12   See 20
14,2   Still unfair? (3,4,3)
16   Fish for X? (3)
17   Fairy face of piece of fungus (8)
19   Neologism when just back at school? (3,4)

21 Singular offal for hospital department on line (7)
22 Private transport carries tropical fish (5)
24 Love-child left out of Bromley's situation (2-3)
25 A day is enough (for the factory?) (5)
27 Tree for tray (3)

Solutions to asterisked clues are contributors to a recipe; clues may be more to their contributions than to themselves.

ACROSS

1 Where it is not 30, say (5)
*4 Go in with wool (3)
6 Beans – every other is ground (5)
9 Warning about America: it went back into the old home producing an effect (9)
10 Fillet grass dweller (5)
*11 Sailor in the present has blood (6)
12 Little old woman rested when Greg cut in (7)
*14 There's nothing in a little venom (4)
*15 Relative to the above's toe (4)
*16 Gall butter (4)
*18 Eat voraciously with tooth (4)
19 See 30
*20 Eye relative to two above (4)
24 Law man and woman to refrain (7)
*26 Method of hiring 27 (6)
28 Subject spelt with an A, which is a very bad thing (5)
29 Leader to lead right one twice misled (9)
*30,19 It's slow to sting (5-4)
*31 Pursue with tongue (3)
*32 Night burner's entrails could be unco hard (5)

DOWN

1 Wine cask almost a pipe (7)
2 Digital sketch? (9)
*3 Continue wearisomely to scale (6)
*4 Lancing candidate to cook thus (4)
5 Divines when heroes got left out (10)
6 Little boy swallowed by insect next (6)
*7 Quiet ship ... on the salt sea (5)
8 Produce of African tree from sun heat (4,3)
13 Gordon and Frank 1 across in industrial area (10)
17 Finished with porkies? It's dangerous for baby (9)
18 What bus will take you to the laundry? (7)

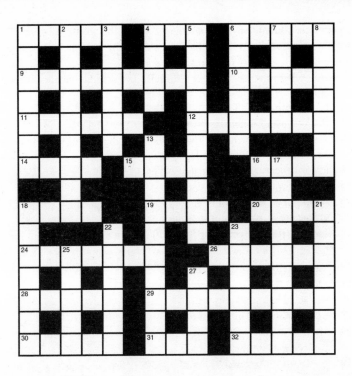

21 Nominal bird, posh one, tailless (7)
*22 Leg furthest South (6)
23 Firm's sulky attitude is an evasion (3-3)
25 Odoriferous openings of elephants and mice (5)
27 Good to succeed – success keeps one up (4)

The perimeter consists of two buildings of which the creator was proud, one across the top and down the right-hand side (9,5), the other down the left and across the bottom (8,6). Remaining solutions are to go in the diagram jigsaw-wise, wherever they will go. Clues are listed in alphabetical order of their solutions.

1 Die – nearly, not quite – when turning up an epic (6)
2 Not a defence to heavy artillery? (8)
3 We hail revolution but not for ever (6)
4 Senior officer taking most of bowl gets a belting (8)
5 Fish with a tail (4)
6 The point of a spittoon? (4)
7 Noises off in Nicosia? (6)
8 Coming from the cold, spy (if quiet) is a mine of information (6,4)
9 Precaution for the winter, marvellous about a month back (3,3)
10 Keats's musk rose: display provocatively outside youth hostel (3,5)
11 Chap heard to take the floor with direction (8)
12 See 13
13,12 Is theatrical Peter dolichocephalic like the perimeter? (8,4)
14 Given 11 for notice about record (6)
15 Picture for setter to study (4)
16 Honey on trial related to the perimeter (10)
17 Common sense about article on a small town in Northern Greece (6)
18 Funny things related to the perimeter? (6)
19 Reported refusal by German island of a quarter-yard (4-4)
20 Dramatic trysting place (as stated) for start of 9 and end of 2 (6,4)
21 The British summer in an aria? (3,4,3)
22 Biblical character of Potiphar, I seem to recall (8)
23 Allude without point to joint (6)
24 Ruled heartlessly and got checked (6)
25 Ruler's got quality – about time (6)
26 Quality of quality, all changed at the third (8)
27 Agreement that may be private (6)
28 Was unaccustomed to work with nude models (6)

ACROSS

1 Tea for the cider drinkers, say? (4,3)
5 Ascribe malpractice to Italian city (7)
9 20 loved 21 and married 16; 16 married 16 21 and 29 20 – the wheel that turned full circle? (9)
10 Bird, Dickensian, with sex appeal (5)
11 One that left the nest for 1 down? (4)
12 8's tenant's husband, a fellow in pink? (10)
14 Bit of a comb for the face by the basin? (5,3)
16 Return of negatives (6)
19 Flowers for St John, also called 11 (6)
20 Gets paid with 18's fruit (8)
21 Features of the landscape otherwise nameless? (10)
23 Nimble one with flowers (4)
26 Food for journey Eastward (5)
27 Sculptor to back an agreement to keep mouth shut? (9)
28 20 the deer on the meadow (7)
29 20 the runner with the weight (7)

DOWN

1 Lost sight of city? (9)
2 Effect of stray wolf (5)
3 Vegetable audibly infringing confidentiality (4)
4 Long tale by original American philosopher (8)
5 Brussels doctor dropping on Actor Jeremy (5)
6 Enlargements cause Spooner to cut payments to the retired (10)
7 Old Afrikaans song including turn on the pedals (4,5)
8 Continue to play the constitutional historian (5)
13 Hanger – building with any of our three authors (6,4)
15 Forestalling of 6 in taboo organisation (9)
17 Just arrived? Take back into Cornish town (5,4)
18 Bird which got involved with fan (8)
21 Something wrong? Thumbs up! (5)
22 Having a lot of shelves makes student nervous (5)
24 1 down's guide dog? (5)
25 Skylight? I don't believe it's coming up (4)

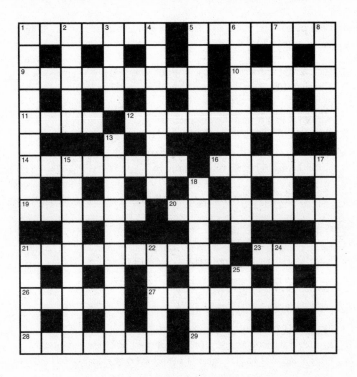

Around the perimeter, clockwise from the top left-hand corner, is the nature of the lease on 9 (4,2,1,8,2,7,4).

1   Listen to commercials with a cutting edge (4)
2   Excellent! Bottom's grabbed Pyramus – leading part; maybe it will create a vacuum (3-4)
3   A pound in a round: I want melanin (6)
4   Plant-fixing cell in church to open book (7,3)
5   Pronouncement of guilt with assurance (10)
6   Crow heard in Northamptonshire (6)
7   Meredith's work, say, to 'eave up (6)
8   Name Austen's work backing French articles (spelt differently by 14) (8)
9   'This …, this …, this ——' (7)
10 Little backing in battle – no tolls here (7)
11 Explosion of some 500 tiger moths (10)
12 Safety device at home to make tea? (6)
13 This led some to be 26'd for 9 (4)
14 Philosopher king with hill-dweller (4)
15 Fragrant shrub to finish in seaweed (8)
16 Principal with detached retina: he should be keeping up (10)
17 Herculean task to put lighting round average distance in China (6,4)
18 Lunch break job – everyone wrong? (6)
19 Go too far, bowling with pace (8)
20 This twice 9? Display contains 13s (8)
21 Possibly poled a boat (there is an easier way) (6)
22 Good appreciative noise for no 1? (4)
23 Bring up from the back (4)
24 Bottom enters authentic defence (8)
25 Peter's penny makes Tom score (4-4)
26 Some doubtful about royal symbol (7)
27 This occurs coming off the pill (10)
28 Electrical unit repeated by insurgents? (4)

ACROSS

9 Little old coin of fop, say, and fool (9)

10,25 Whereat possible clue leads to enemy 2 27 4 (5,7)

11 Put in case wife gets at husband? (7)

12,20 24 15's soldier backed no happy current (7,6)

13 Boy with flag to get out (5)

14 Drive when on the left with chief support (5-4)

15 See 24

19 Cockney nurse, one giving relief around (9)

22 It's legitimate to be beheaded, which is shocking (5)

24,15 Not only did they not append a large number but two Thomases penned it (3,4,3,7,5)

25 See 10

26 Monarch who was shot to give us cover, they say (5)

27 See 2

DOWN

1 A divine drink makes sense (4,2)

2,27,4 Gee! (he re-wrote) untrodden way with words of William and Thomas (5,3,9,4)

3 Enemy 2 27 4 helps to show interest (6)

4 See 2

5 Halo (if split) of pearls? (6)

6 Endless Gallic circumvention of tiebreak is mad (8)

7 Polish supporter of English composer (6)

8 Confidential documents may be like wheat (8)

14,17 Heater – no right to use Welsh forest (6)

15 Plant 2 4 for model with joint name (4,4)

16 Nurse may deal with circulation problem (8)

17 See 14

18 Spur to miss target? (8)

20 See 12

21 Injury a barrier to getting old? (6)

22 Depart with a boast (6)

23 A number are the same in Texas (6)

25 Undesirable in the garden to be thus watered? (4)

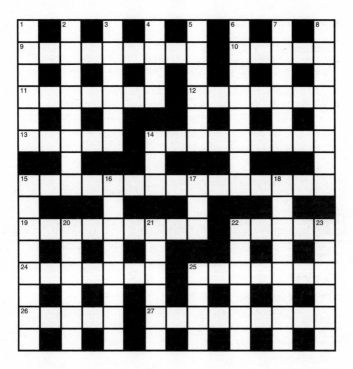

Theme words are asterisked.

ACROSS

*1 Smoker who fiddled with cocaine finds playwright Antony –
    philosopher John's holding actor Ian (8,6)

9 Money for tobacco (4)

*10 Creature from the King's Head killed Fitzroy McPherson (5,4)

12 Advocate of co-operation, not wise unfortunately (7)

13 Film bird on burner in the Lakes (7)

14 Patron called upon to provide tips for division (5)

*15 Eyesore, unusually blue, found in goose (9)

*18 Carrot topped in league that copied out the Encyclopaedia (3-6)

*21 Tom the engineer's lost property (5)

22 Leave some musicians performing? (7)

25 Posh politician aged under twenty or probably a lot more (7)

26 Vendor in various galleries, South not East (5,4)

27 Job for Christmas? (4)

*28 Mr Jonas Oldacre discovered blood round wire (7,7)

DOWN

*2 Tenancy, in a word? 'It is a nice —— … that is the baboon'
    (The 8) (9)

*3 Group 'allied to the old Carbonari's' left ring (3,6)

4 Ducks alighted first on top of church made of grainy limestone (7)

5 Adverse critic on the door (7)

6 Nothing like islands – or is it? (5)

7 Rendering of 'My way' – neighbouring Keys? (5)

*8 Gamble on monarch-fronted group producing a swamp-adder (8,4)

*11 Sidekick in indoor court heard question as to the programme (6,6)

16 Put in clay which is strangely out of character (9)

17 Attracted her attention, they say – fire away! (9)

19 Pope's brown sleuths getting round article (7)

20 From where the coloured French used in Equus? (6-1)

*23 'The woman' psychiatrist (5)

24 Princess's firm does recordings (5)

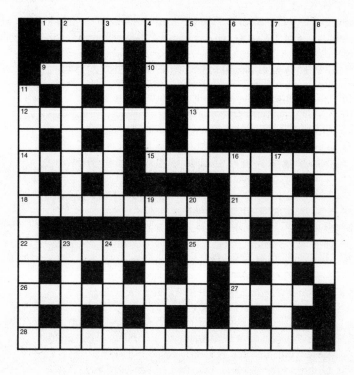

Perimeter, clockwise from the top left-hand corner: To the mind of the hero, though —— (6,4,3,2,3,6,4), the revel was a 4 10 8-ed in the non-14. Remaining clues must be fitted into the diagram jigsaw-wise, wherever they will go. Their clues are listed in alphabetical order of the solutions.

1 Counselling is what's wrong with our epoch (6)
2 Courage is a true support (7)
3 Meeting to determine what is the done thing? (10)
4 The thing that is done by the cat of the copper (6)
5 Scattering of seed in which to meet up with the 8-ed (8)
6 The science of managing itches? (6)
7 Canines, as a setter, say, with effective powers (3,5)
8 Official appreciation of number in time (6)
9 It joins points of graphic equality when I replace Georgia in petrol (7)
10 Sir Thomas's addition (4)
11 I agree to go to sleep (6)
12 When Benvolio's half confused with 10 (8)
13 Sum union produces is awful (8)
14 A verb's needed in 'Once 10 into the ——'? The opposite … (10)
15 Be too strong for a Parisian after love and its awful tug (6)
16 Love (verb, archaic), as Hecate called the witches (8)
17 Girl from the Winter's Tale (pirated edition) (7)
18 Left to rise shakily on report of a fight (8)
19 Right with propeller for part of Lion's part (4)
20 Cuttings – remove weeds with old flipflop? (4-4)
21 Six-footer perhaps, but reportedly fought with Joan of Arc (6)
22 Singularly large amount in excessive leave-taking (6-2)
23 Some affect remorse at a bit of a shake-up (6)
24 Antony was one to make much of his success against the Irish (8)
25 Heroine's relation: pity to lose relation to European seaman? (6)
26 One soul may be set free (7)
27 Hero's wife, not quite a maid, returning to be sick (8)
28 6 take much of the day's goodness (6)

Perimeter: Odd ad for computer firm – Almost his? The very idea's utterly absurd (3,6,7,4,5,3). Remaining solutions are to go in the diagram jigsaw-wise, wherever they will go. Clues are listed in alphabetical order of their solutions.

1 Every other old sub's missing officer (6)
2 Plant secreting oil for article in song (7)
3 One changing colour sounds on the way out (4)
4 Outpouring of English by Welsh girl embracing American (8)
5 Prince on strike in Sheffield (6)
6 Danish prince, good runner, has a laugh about a judge (8)
7 Dripstones form undesirable growth among thugs (4-6)
8 Eminem's topless work, if not Araucaria's – hence the perimeter (2,8)
9 Writer's tips include 'Idiom is rum? Change it' (10)
10 Submediants lash out (4)
11 Salad for drunk from Riga (7)
12 Quality of perimeter: no monster – here? (10)
13 Annie who shot at a tree on the meadow (6)
14 Larger base for height producing coal with 11 (5,5)
15 King in Rockingham (for example) is unchanged in a hide (6)
16 No one here to play with Italian girl, and no play centre (7)
17 Shove – not yet? (4)
18 Greek speakers (shorter version) (7)
19 Spotted bay tree with centre removed (4)
20 Fruit of Scottish blackthorn for sale (4)
21 Meal on plate is duck (4)
22 Wimbledon being broadcast? He wrote 8 for 5 (8)
23 Avenue, or half of one? No logging over this (4,4)
24 Wavy one of French section of … (4)
25 … slip in it doesn't say when (deserving better marks) (10)
26 Unable to see lunatic is in love with saints (10)
27 In fives, gold rings where Johnny came down to Soviet marshal (10)
28 Go off course Northwards, result of bore (4)

The perimeter is the question answered above: where? 10 (no good) the 5 (part 2)s 6 (4,3,2,5,3,5,3,3).

1   Help rating traveller (4)
2   Life before death, they say: 'ere's custom for the church (1,5)
3   Publicise industrial actions or aggressive flights (3,7)
4   Charm coming across on top of tree (6)
5   Unreliable consequence of perimetrical activity (6,4)
6   How Middlesex and Surrey are split from Herbert and Ivy? (2,3,5)
7   Overconfident commander goes to Kings in remedy (8)
8   Trustworthy band peeled off (10)
9   Never mind the land sticking out into the river (7)
10 … prime number for the street? (7)
11 Celebration by anti-revolutionary known to St Paul (8)
12 The fellow's going to the inferno (4)
13 Reluctant start for gay lover (4)
14 Runner in Falstaff's last speech nearly got back when daughter got in (5,3)
15 Refusal to turn aside keeps doctor in dreary period (8)
16 Golden seal and golden wrath returns as well (6-4)
17 Aquatic feature of Wath upon Dearne (4)
18 As far as other things are concerned they serve to earth lessons (6)
19 Unusual science for unusual race (6)
20 One of two houses, largely Jewish (4)
21 Addressed Umbrian city with central character going back one (5,2)
22 Well dweller badly placed in draw (6)
23 Left winger keeping order over setter's gibberish (8)
24 Motor vehicle reversing decay to horsedrawn one (7)
25 The word with war is money (4)
26 No boiler for department who act badly (7,3)
27 Having one's feet under the table, say, in a flowery place (6)
28 Jolly break amid lamentation provided by aerator (8)

In the hatched squares are the missing words in the following quotation:
'—— (6) hath —— (8,5), and therefore —— (6) shall —— (5,2,4),
Macbeth shall —— (5,2,4)'. Remaining solutions are to go in the diagram
jigsaw-wise, wherever they will go. Clues are listed in alphabetical order of
their solutions.

1 A sign of direction (6)
2 Bill's quality too early for the quote (3,3)
3 Cushion for a returning angel, mostly (6)
4 Epithet for God on Panorama? (3-6)
5 French boy in the 'grand refusal' (5)
6 Give job to Hal's pal – detail in appropriate setting (7)
7 Driver in the sky embracing she-goat (6)
8 Seat for animal doctor in cure (9)
9 Snout having nothing to drink, only stones (3,4)
10 Summary of item Poe edited (7)
11 Queen contracted fungal disease (5)
12 Clear what used to be a single standard (9)
13 Clones reportedly used by burglar? (6)
14 They are instrumental in taking ti with sugar (7)
15 Chief stableman good in space over 6ft? (4,5)
16 Find lie diffused by unbeliever (7)
17 Awfully leaky sort of pin (5)
18 Clue or D in Cornwall (5,3)
19 Reduce oral teaching? (6)
20 Song of the cuckoo has capital learner (8)
21 Spanish relative found in Northern island – that would be telling (9)
22 Sihanouk who stepped down a month back without punishment (7)
23 Actor on hand with dates? (4,4)
24 Fairy horse nearest to earth (7)
25 Game for start of day in another year (5)
26 Season and/or reason? (5)
27 Poet laureate holds back poem in which Queen speaks of
   herself (5,2)
28 Dickens villain embracing Burney heroine starts as a riddle (5-4)
29 Arm may be inside and heart outside (6)

30 Confectioner's folds: hope not the end (4,4)
31 International organisation ends with smalls (6)
32 Unknown food for poet (5)

Perimeter, clockwise *from the dotted square*: Following 10's lethal exposure, unmasked spy fled. Yours, Wordsworth (3,3,6,6,2,3,5).

1   Did what was required to the morning dew, like the sky (say) on a road (4,4)
2   Cronin's work has made a little appearance in the French sky (7)
3   French boy could be nearly nineteen (7)
4   Araucaria had briefly been heard and seen (4)
5   Hearing of complaint was in the air (4)
6   Weirdo saw it in the paper, it's said – it's without interest (4,6)
7   Stuffy English cricketer (CB) keeping wicket in Australia (6)
8   Criminal poet (4)
9   Small resident rhymer (5,5)
10 Poppy's follower and fellow monster (detail) by painter (10)
11 Poem by bad hat precedes enquiry about location of sting (1,5)
12 Earth's song rendered in place of Manet's Lunch (2,3,5)
13 Cornish painter nearly consumed one of the perimeter (6)
14 Amorous other ranks asked for more music (6)
15 Too bad about the pit containing the perimeter (7)
16 Scottish magpie comes in to copy other birds (4)
17 Tribal magician needed when the Sun has covered outside court (4-6)
18 Poor Celeste in danger of being chosen again (10)
19 Ingenuity is expedient (8)
20 Give a good smooth finish to a West Midlands district (8)
21 Your health is grand in the Sun (4)
22 Purpose of perimeter: clear wet snow with Spooner's broom? (5,5)
23 Islington spirit whose last article punctures dialectician (3,5)
24 Yarns about Englishman, property of elbow straightener (5,5)
25 Bird's enemy (4)
26 Topped like a potato yielding lots of milk (7)
27 Lament for small copper (4)
28 Speedwell (the flower) (4)

ACROSS

1 Draw name and place (4)
3 Runs society for ordinary people (8)
8 See 22
10 Early feminist, about to join the majority, wanting even more (8)
11 Danger line? According to 22 8, each 12dn 1ac possessed two 14s, three ——s, ... (5)
12 ... ten 28s, fifteen ——s, a 26, and a 4 (Buzzer to sound reveille round hospital) (4-5)
13 Ring for student dropping note and retaining the next one down (7)
14 Get information from footwear (4)
17 Energy you pay for when you get it? It isn't plain speaking (4)
19 Italian writer Dante losing fat (keeping a bit of it) (7)
23 Discrimination possibly to do with stage (4,5)
24,5 22 8's alternative hero, of good standing in novel by morning (5,7)
25 Ultra detailed Latinism in which people are dying (8)
26 Bumble, inwardly an unlikely lad? (6)
27 Scatcherd in 22 8 could lead us a dance (3,5)
28 Work talk don't talk work (4)

DOWN

1 New Year in Vietnam rather cold (said with irritation) (8)
2 Conflict of two roses with 17 (8)
4 Hub of Western civilisation, endless serving of mackerel pâté (11)
5 See 24
6 Help in flower, in short, in bed (4,2)
7 Good person to see about genealogy, having credibility? (6)
9 Synthetic city and a half (5)
12 Pub groups to let in 'purely agricultural' county (11)
15 Have to change about 100 cents in covered area (8)
16 Thumb raised for tonic (4-2-2)
18 Active personality after period without leader (2,3,2)
20 Will comedian sound like Scots kingdom? (5)
21 Way out black girl losing head (6)
22,8 Novel hero from 17 playing wrong instrument inside (6,6)

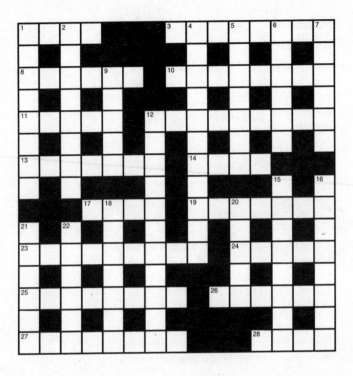

The perimeter with 20 for 28 is an examiner's addition to Wordsworth's question to the cuckoo (5,3,11,9).

1 A cast almost beyond the pale? (4)
2 Little deer gets a V-sign thanks to one coming in (10)
3 Headpieces were current among intelligent Americans (6)
4 Downing's record in mayonnaise? (10)
5 Cure is tardy with students involved (3-4)
6 Same again from the choir (4)
7 Selfish boy about to leave little money (10)
8 New counsellor dropping those same students to avoid monochrome (8)
9 Leg you broke at funeral ? (6)
10 Coin used by neurologists (4)
11 Pieces taken from Royal entering bar first (8)
12 Tall characters in the end don't change or die (8)
13 Social occasion following wild drive? (4,4)
14 Breakfast on oat? (4)
15 Opinion poll with memento (4)
16 Doctor, brilliant achiever, in Bosnia (6)
17 Dancer opposed to look at series returning (7)
18 West Yorkshire town (Caucasian model) for big badgers? (6)
19 Minimum money gives girl tranquillity, they say (5-5)
20 Thinks (see preamble) (7)
21 Pretend I'm nothing requiring rescue (10)
22 Old rake, heartless villain (4)
23 Certain to heal oneself? (6)
24 Clare with climber on brief flight, not an easy ball to hit? (5,3)
25 Expedition catching fish in troubled sea (4,3)
26 Rioted wildly when transistor replaced it? (6)
27 Report of essay taking vast amounts of paper in old ships (8)
28 6 topped among solvers with grains (see preamble) (4,6)

Perimeter: Eponymous hero's boast: Lambert gives his name as Polaris (1,2,8,2,3,8,4). Remaining solutions are to go in the diagram jigsaw-wise, wherever they will go. Clues are listed in alphabetical order of their solutions.

1 Brown fellow, nearly all male (6)
2 Characters giving sacred river help (8)
3 See 16
4 Lake in Libra (4)
5 Trinket is black with a blue variant (6)
6 American cannabis-type plant in osteopathy? (7)
7 Suffered loudly when brought into the world (4)
8 The real hero was not a tram, being outside the groove (6)
9 Legendary king, no gentleman, gets awfully raw deal (10)
10 8's mate lives, turned into his reason (for the war) (7)
11 Assembly of manor tenants from Truro (Bacon) (5-5)
12 Facility of feminine ending without a relation (8)
13 Healthy return here by David from giant-killing (4)
14 Draw out about tenpence as stated (8)
15 What the Lord said (and Baroness Orczy wrote) on getting a loan? (1,4,5)
16,3 German part of Switzerland held by girl friend of hero (4,6)
17 Back Russian entry to sail (8)
18 Prince's associate quietly takes him to former Tory leader with admirals and painted ladies (10)
19 Wartime activities in the theatre (10)
20 Scarf, article in where it's sociable to do business (10)
21 Types like this could paint (7)
22 Article (not leader) about one bereaved (6)
23 Do wrong again, getting at a drink (8)
24 Stick in painter's country (6)
25 The isle (in Shakespeare's first song) is full of noise (8)
26 House partly on motorway (4)
27 Broadcasts special books (7)
28 War scene with weight (4)

Perimeter: Part of 11's lament – what then to add? Wretched motor knocking? (4,3-6,6,2,3,4). Remaining solutions are to go in the diagram jigsaw-wise, wherever they will go. Clues are listed in alphabetical order of their solutions.

1   Capone was false? Close (6)
2   Dress on a car, say? (6)
3   Almost make a difference to one in WW2 POW camp (6)
4   Put out? Here's some money back on English canned soup (15)
5   Questions of right and wrong settled by itches (6)
6   Questions of good and ill left in the open (6)
7   Greek inferno hardly nice (8)
8   Keep Lent and don't give up? (4,4)
9   Home expert at a meeting (6)
10 Make an insertion in boneless instrument with it (8)
11 104900 mph? (6)
12 Want fish for making cross? (8)
13 Recycling trash one can produce a supply of gas (5,3)
14 Eye-spots round string player? No way (6)
15 Type of tape recorder for peer – Lone Ranger? (4-4)
16 Fabric to make instrument cease to sound (8)
17 Broken toe constrains wader: pull it to tell marines? (5,3)
18 Leisure activities are supposed to engineer start of action in Greek island (8)
19 Maybe watch one having traveller for breakfast? (8)
20 Report hardwood more expensive? Could be a storm here (6)
21 Spy in the cricket field (5,3)
22 Doin' mechanical writin', say, going through 'The Shirt'? (6)
23 Drum for little boy at French dance (6)
24 Change of script in 'Last train to … er …' (error) (15)
25 Wobbly Miss, later Mrs Thorne, beheaded (8)
26 Andy doing converse of piecework? (6)

Across clues are quotations from Shakespeare, and the solutions are the speakers. Downs are normal.

ACROSS

1 I'll find a day to massacre them all (6)
4 His bloody brow! O Jupiter! No blood (8)
10 Hearing thy mildness praised in every town ... Myself am moved to woo thee for my wife (9)
11 Then set before my face the lord Aumerle (5)
12 Well said: that was laid on with a trowel (5)
13 O thou foul thief! Where hast thou stowed my daughter? (9)
14 No, sir, I do not bite my thumb at you, sir (7)
16 My father, in his habit as he lived (6)
19 Must you with hot irons burn out both mine eyes? (6)
21 Pluck out his eyes (7)
23 For her own person, it beggared all description (9)
25 Will you go hunt, my lord? (5)
27 Full of vexation come I, with complaint against my child (5)
28 There is nothing left remarkable beneath the visiting moon (9)
29 Not in love neither? Then let's say you are sad because you are not merry (8)
30 O thou, mine heir ... what strange fish hath made his meal on thee? (6)

DOWN

1 Playing as usual with the petty cash, last out (8)
2 Some talk – not all – of Ophelia as more attractive (5)
3 Royal fellow's entering painful cry in North Rhine dialect (9)
5 Anywhere here is just as deep: that's how I do my ablutions (7)
6 Talk with bachelor of heavy beat (for cricketers in Oz) (5)
7 A long way from which to get Hilary? (5-4)
8 Start of play continuing in court? (6)
9 Greek article on prohibition (6)
15 Hard and polished American defence during dinner, say (9)
17 German city endlessly leading one friend with relation to it? (9)
18 Where Keats had much travelled, loaded or otherwise? (8)
20 Polish image of cross here? (7)
21 Acquire, without request, a seal (6)

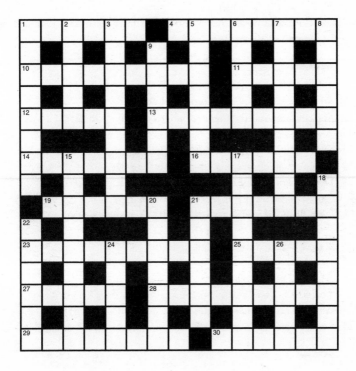

22 Holiday hole (6)
24 Goose is nearly the solution (5)
26 I leave a share to desert (3,2)

Asterisked clues may be as unconventional as their solutions, of which only those in the first verse were explained.

ACROSS

  *1 Talk fast, said the cooker (10)

*6,20 Stray pig with stray ma (mother) (4,4)

  9 Spoken acknowledgement of where vanishing cat sat (5)

*10 Animated cleaner lookalikes address boss in waves (9)

*12 Don't talk for the last and first at the gallery (just a thought) (6)

*13 Strange women keeping strange job for a day (8)

 14 Don't acknowledge return of food (4)

 16 One volume I left is incised and polished (9)

*18 Urge to move round bone like 6,20 (it's my own invention) (9)

 20 See 6

*23 What 30 were doing making holes (8)

 24 City sacked by Poles with army (6)

 27 Bird for Brother William with commercial break (9)

 28 Chaps jolly good at bridge? (5)

*29 What 30 did in the revolution? (4)

*30 Cheese eater born in mid-4 (solve it without solver's work) (6,4)

DOWN

  *1 Bird with its head among a lot of sweets (6)

  2 Fish, almost unsighted, keeping up fire over the water (7)

  3 Code giving direction to sceptic? (5)

  *4 26 around timepiece with president (4)

  5 Message with flower for motorist (3,6)

  7 Died on the fifth with debts on patent (7)

  8 Some disturbance arising during leisure, not the one with the story (4,4)

 11 One who eats turkey? (7)

*15 Produced blood from stone topped up first as 1ac did (7)

 16 A drinking bout cut short amid bunting by one on board with the Midshipmaid? (5,4)

 17 Supply horse, say, maybe bay, good for takeaway food (5-3)

 19 ANC leader, original, with Drum (7)

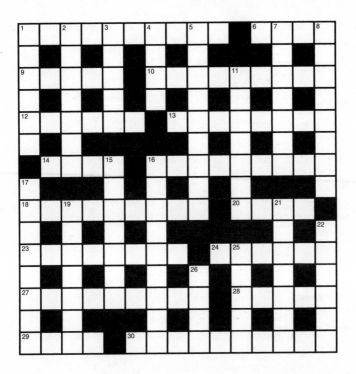

21 Volunteers fled to Italian port (7)
22 Numbered puzzle heroine with quality of cat? (6)
*25 Setter's accepting one text for portmanteau (5)
26 4 is always getting lost (4)

ACROSS

1 Make up to hills, make up to plain, starting all together (2,3,4,5)
10,8,18 Merchant's market died: he typically destroyed 1, the whole family of 20 (3,2,6,8,3,5,3)
11 See NHS man accepting complete revolutionary (6,3)
12 See 19
13 'A bird unto the hill' it appears (6)
15 All is not all, they tell me (3)
17 Finch keeps captive in charge of rock from snake (11)
18 See 10
21 'Shoe' used to be pronounced 'she' (3)
22 Oriental fellow to eat noisily? (6)
23 I won't fight to cover topless tribe with top (8)
26 Former perfume is becoming hard to find (9)
27 Jack's wedding? (5)
28 Use mirror in error: I'm not taking you to the door! (3,8,3)

DOWN

2 Topless flower girl turned up at the ends (5)
3 Deaths by drowning for those who oppose keeping up 24 hours (7)
4 What leads one astray is, after all, led astray (5,5)
5,25 Painter or successful lookout on voyage? (8)
6 Perform degrading task in space around bend on river (4,3)
7 Implied meanings or explicit meanings? (9)
8 See 10
9 White men from un-American wonderland race as one man upset drinks (9,5)
14 Top or bottom of the necropolis? (4,6)
16 Road with eating area for shop girl in Paris (9)
19,12 20's denial of his enemy's paternity (2,3,2,8)
20 Fifer gets warmer keeping a record (7)
24 Rate of unemployment in an air-umbrella (5)
25 See 5

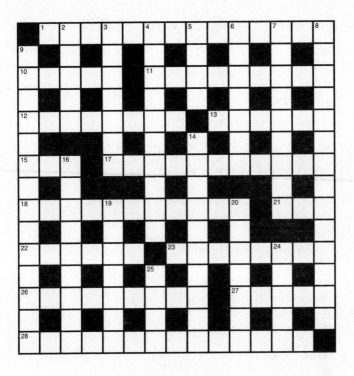

JB might be clued as 'Work with craft keeps globe turning round' (6,4).

ACROSS

1   Message about damaged mail: it's covered by insurance (9)
6,10   A JB hero, I follow Kirk changing gear both ways at centre of gravity (5-5-4)
9   Being drawn into a quarter (2,3)
10   See 6
11   Pike, sick inside, has female name (7)
12   Remaining pictures after half-time? (7)
13   Virgil's love for a peacock in JB (4)
14   I love a big hole in (sic) with similar skylights (10)
18   Port with a JB beast in an uproar (10)
19   Soon unidentifiable? (4)
21   Suffers more pieces of river (7)
24   One produced by American Mozart? (7)
26   Don't talk – hearken afresh to JB beast (5,4)
27   Words of address used so far (2,3)
28   A drink at a play (5)
29   JB beasts and retired painter in on-line piece (6-3)

DOWN

1   JB's kite left in the cold (5)
2   Carol shot in error: here they hope to be hung (3,6)
3   JB's alien cut by tailless dormouse (6)
4   Flour and eggs with water and salt on the South Bank (9)
5   River – Eastern one – forming ridge from glacier (5)
6   Mrs Annie Turner's proficient on a horse (8)
7   JB's reptile, a bachelor in a sacred building (5)
8   Collection of local words in a stupid picture (9)
13   Made pithy remarks, imitated when man's keeping gold inside (9)
15   Man of the past century taking most of Italian region on (3-6)
16   Carol's amount of hay requires use of flame gun, right? (9)
17   JB's beast's total prey – he needs time (8)
20   Stories of JB's reptile and his wife, not one with cattle disease (6)
22   JB's beast from Lakeland (5)
23   Gentleman from South Africa with Irishman from Edinburgh? (5)
25   Where no sound is heard on the floor? 'Who cares?', I say (5)

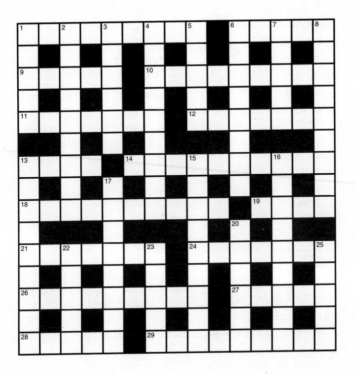

24 The Girl in the Badger's

---

* I have taken the liberty of spelling this as most of us literary ignoramuses naturally would; TS himself omitted the E.

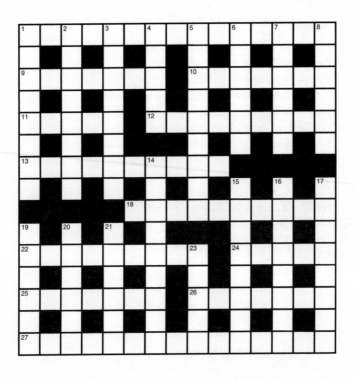

ACROSS

1 Planner of 9 26, a remarkably sane tale (8)
6 Big fair bird? (6)
9,26 6 2's work from 4 zero – they use string (3,5,8)
10 Perform a trick that is uninteresting when put back inside (6)
11 This number'd brought courage to Americans, they say (5-3)
12 Go back into tent for dairy product (6)
13 Friend to leave? Must be a lie! (5)
15 Bilingual invocation for cages where I change case and return (3,4)
17 Additional payment, about a shilling, for large wild ox (7)
19,23 First of 9 26 gets guidance in school time: I signal to actor (5,8)
21 His Highness abandons merry German caper (6)
23 See 19
25 Bush makes Alcoholics Anonymous drunk with milk (6)
26 See 9
27 Deity heartless? Pray about Newport (6)
28 Such a university dangerous but trusty character? (8)

DOWN

2 See 6
3 Date to —— the patience of a ——? (5)
4 Problems of identity in quotes with a solution (9)
5 Stories about soldier and deserving persons getting a tumour (7)
6,2 Flower and tree, passage authorised at 9 26 (5,7)
7 Happy girl distraught when I leave without love – I'll tell you if she lies (9)
8 Foreign articles on last year's leaders: 'Mr 1 was an —— man of 11' … (7)
14 … and 'not quite a —— but you would hardly notice it' (Cherry, keeping Thaw's name back) (9)
16 Bird is in flower raised to be made immortal (9)
17,22 The other of 9 26: sailors in proper adornment caught bird (7,5)
18 Boy with recipe for eggs used for tea (7)
20 Not a mountainous journey, they tell us, to Toulouse (7)
22 See 17
24 Season doesn't start with place in earth (5)

The shaded squares were followed by Ferdinand, with their burden (4,4,3, 5-4,4: 3,3). Remaining solutions are to go in the diagram jigsaw-wise, wherever they will go. Clues are listed in alphabetical order of their solutions.

1 Original patriarch with a second sacrifice? (5)
2 Disease in spiked shoe? (8,4)
3 Joe heard on the internet? (6)
4 The British Leyland cycle was incapable (6)
5 Reported beater as original killer (4)
6 Too select to make a national stage (9)
7 Sing about English perfume to many in the first quarter (8,4)
8 Bandit has a business getting into his second part (6)
9 Night flier, say, to provide weapons to invade barbarian (5,4)
10 Elicit agreement with woman about (5)
11 A feeling unfit for a party (4,4)
12 Pain can be nourishing if it's this (6)
13 Part of an additive makes a surplus for a friend (9)
14 Become mature student (comment of friend) (5)
15 Superior sound of the never? (6)
16 Red dye made by meerkats at departing (6)
17 Most of 12 dictionary is about church name being given to theft (9)
18 Most extensive art having cravings (7)
19 Bugbear making some progress (4)
20 Cross-grained little Jack dropping top on your head (6)
21 Apply another match to some items missing as a rule (5)
22 Plangent note, golden in a sense (8)
23 Holy person's craving for minimum clothing? (6)
24 Firewater can be death to insects (6)
25 Time for bird to encourage horse? (6)
26 Two points is a score and a half! (6)
27 Barber's soon at sea in test (9)
28 Speaker's pretty-pretty piece of territory (7)
29 Strips – it's awfully hot – among family members (9)
30 Vessel about to have back what hasn't been put on (6)

Across the top and bottom lines of the perimeter go a loveless father and daughter, and down the sides go a son and mother from the same play.

1 Sect is disbanded in summit: how long will it take to retrieve? (6,4)
2 Unfortunately society has abandoned a girl (4)
3 Stamina with deer playing heartless music (10)
4 Brother of father is worker on 10 (7)
5 'Thisby, the flowers have odious savours sweet', for example, is what really matters (6,4)
6 Blush to see old city in putsch (6,2)
7 Little boy passes on and goes round (6)
8 Advantage is indeed general (4)
9 Case alien to both of us, say? (4)
10 Regular time for poets (4)
11 Celebration knight had missed (4)
12 One with two ears according to etymology which is stupid (7)
13 Grub heard to be hot stuff (4)
14 Novel lady we hate to be a pioneer (4,3,3)
15 Plant part with single seed, fresh and admirable, as the Americans say (6)
16 Test for care if past (4)
17 Money without climbing aid is a plague (10)
18 Water table game? (4)
19 Essential backing in Eire's arrangement to eliminate the absolute? (10)
20 Farceur keeping change of value from abbey (8)
21 Dress for a capital (4)
22 Nice area for classical man returned first time (7)
23 Our turn for naval battle with sheep station worker (10)
24 Teacher's way to accost his pupil? (10)
25 First character in our play to achieve right emphasis (10)
26 Not having much … money? (but plenty of butter, one hopes) (10)
27 Shakespeare's first play (keeping silence!) is ostentatious (7)
28 Creator of Bond causes row (4)

Linked solutions have partial clues.

ACROSS

1,28,13	Suppress intelligence, keeping painting in church (6,10)
3	See 24
9	Destination of handiwork, large quantities eaten by dog (5,4)
10	Beg him not to grant link with 5, 27 and other joined up solutions (5)
11,23	Mister maintaining himself in Ankara in the clutches of Fogg's other half (6,3,3)
12	Put under amid danger signal (8)
14	In life's feast, Sleep, being murdered, ruins hero (9)
15	See 17
17,15	Isn't it about a king in a shirt? (5,5)
18	A lot of animals inflict curses on their original cells (9)
20	How crown wearers awkwardly lay in use (8)
23	See 11
24,3	Star man with one of force where it's at work (5,11)
25	Reproduction of wren's song strikes false note (9)
27	Know following books about organ? (6,5)
28	See 1

DOWN

1	Spice Boy's ancient city (7)
2	Strengthen river defences with bat (9)
3	What lies between Stratford and Bow, with a lot of game about, is an army camp (9)
4	I'm disgusted by you getting fortune back (3)
5	Journalist to turn cross (5,5)
6	Smithy's fake (5)
7	Churchman's shrub (5)
8	Animal in antiquity raised by general in 'Catch 22' (7)
13	See 1ac
15	Also called silent in missing work – otherwise only called outside (4,5)
16	Sunset – cup broken – they never thought it was me (9)
17	Coming between apprentice and master? Couldn't do otherwise (5,2)

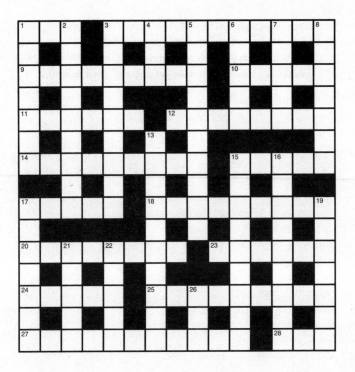

19 Iniquity pursuing its own sphere finally gets lodged in the brain (5,2)

21 Finale of the golden voice (5)

22 Plant for South facing border (5)

26 Timeless notice of death by magic (3)

Perimeter, clockwise from the top left-hand corner: Customs at pub: maybe aged one this month becoming less dense about solution, as Lear saw himself (4,6,7,4,7). Remaining solutions are to go in the diagram jigsaw-wise, wherever they will go. Clues are listed in alphabetical order of their solutions.

1 Like a bird's behind (6)
2 Not the only way of portraying dislike? (8)
3 Dressed as (more or less) a boy (4)
4 Hurry on board with bribe (4)
5 Quitch is a drug withdrawn from bank by fool (3-5)
6 Environmental studies, say, covering effect of cool (unknown) (7)
7 Fell into ecstasy by rapid increase (10)
8 Accessory to begin vegan's conversion (7,3)
9 Note over formerly lively person (4)
10 Morning or evening opening contrived by tradesman (10)
11 Man or no man? (6)
12 One Sienese painter making masonry blocks (7)
13 Type of hospital I can attend (6)
14 Wool for doctor of trichology? (6)
15 Take sodium home to dispose of Highlander (8)
16 Say when? (4,3)
17 Amphibious part of scientist (4)
18 Failure to assert one's rights in new French relation's pointless goal (3-5)
19 I leave instruction for artillery (8)
20 Great house, first in locality (6)
21 Press it afresh and press on regardless (7)
22 Tart up? Old advice: put oxygen in aircraft (10)
23 One is as one turns out, a Slavophil (10)
24 Returning Cleopatra's attendant's dress (4)
25 Girl with youth and not sex appeal in the Mediterranean, say (8)
26 Mistake of a girl? (4)
27 … in which love is seated, holding special people of extreme self-belief (10)
28 Muse of prince in island retreat (6)

The books have the same source.

ACROSS

8 Cloak effect of falling (6)

9,20,22 Book recently come of age, old style (8-6-4)

10 Beautiful world for 2 6 (8)

11 The Cheshire sleuth (6)

12 See 3

14 After election I go West from East as a young swimmer (8)

16 Publicity to head covering article in comparatively inferior book (4,2,5,4)

17 Drink is great problem even swallowed (5,3)

19 Outer for crows (6)

21 Musical theme acknowledged on menu (6)

23 See sea given a makeover (8)

25 Doctor has no port – and no cat (8)

26 A little note (6)

DOWN

1 Where am I? Or are they peaceniks? I don't be*lieve* it! (4,4)

2,6 Screen personality about to lift arms (4,4)

3,15,12 Book 'Duvet et dehors' with Donald non-negotiable (4,3,3,2,5,3,6)

4 Simply another duty policeman with centre-left tendency (15)

5 Book a game with matches with warning about little fellow (6,4)

6 See 2

7 Meaning of applause for student in writer Fay's English (4,4)

13 Musical tube performed – spice girl not perform at all? (10)

15 See 3

18 Think about a boy (6)

20,22 See 9

24 Not enough current for power siren? (4)

31 Flights upon the Banks of Thames

ACROSS

ACROSS

9   Bamboozle us with old rose that has no scent (9)
10   Mapmakers' alias for Eastern city (5)
11   Hamlet'd said he'd condescended (7)
12   They make incursions first into the cavalry (7)
13,8 Sir Hugh was a killer when backing a way to pay for crime (5,6)
14   See 3
16,22dn Blows killer's outlet near play scene (7,6)
18   Look! No clothes on! Picture with 12 (4,3)
20   Did the crossword from hell, ending in divorce? (9)
22   College heard to facilitate entry (5)
23,25 Shallow mere – water frozen – land on it (7,7)
27,28 Such was namesake of poet James beloved by Miss 7 (5,9)

DOWN

1   Passage half the play? (4)
2   Another play or opera missing the entry in British Steel (10)
3,14 In yarn, chips chef cooked for 22 (6,9)
4   Fred's pal went off and made rocks (8)
5   Lost, as a dog? (6)
6   Fellow-little-American fellow of 2 (8)
7   Clue to 1 with fool removed (4)
8   See 13
13   Amazing love between Wests! (3)
15   *Isms* (10)
17   Lack of correspondence with long moment (8)
18   Grey month captured by boy solvers (4,4)
19   Picture of Folkestone (3)
20   Foot from finger (6)
21   Trip gave you endless trouble (6)
22   See 16
24   Extinct ox or disheartened bear (4)
26   Bird of the lough (4)

Pairs of 33s are: be 1, 13; 28, 7ac; 15 17 9, gather 9 10; 5, be a 4dn; 29, 15 17; 14, 31; 29 23, be 30; 11, be a 7dn; 22dn, 25. Most of these are unclued, and the others have partial clues, as have 27, 19, 24 and 16 which are halves of similar pairs.

ACROSS

1 B without oxygen (4)
4 Raise for 30? You cannot be serious (5)
12 Travel one may be taken for (4)
16 Sign of 11 or 2 with setter's backing (7)
18 Liers in wait gain admission to the presidency (6)
20 Some call a trial judge Your Worship (6)
22 Intelligence of woman doesn't last (and isn't wrung?) (7)
24 Little money (4)
26 Journey may be down to earth (4)
30 Aids to reproduction for people like Michael Martin (8)
32 A leap to be plentiful (6)
33 Father bird? (4)
34 Bird with seat for object (5)
35 Cid so written for Christmas? (4)

DOWN

2 Exit result (7)
3 Nasals in month without its historic day that doesn't belong (3-6)
4 Some backing for resolution (5)
6 Garment to disguise goat? (4)
7 Change of heart (5)
8 State students to be hell (7)
15,17 Human jetsam? (8)
19 Analysis could be nervous (9)
21 A place for an oracle in the theatre (7)
27 Would-be incriminating garden item? (5)
31 But not North? (3)

ACROSS

1 Lying with flowers? (2,3)
4 Big ends of ribs? Follow that, Fitzgerald! (9)
9 Soft material for tea on French river (9)
10 Boy running 16? (5)
11 Hanger on hand (4)
12 Gulf home to Scot and maid that played (10)
14 Drink, say, and return medal (6)
15 Island (German) needs organiser (8)
17 Beware these eyes for metal strip on roof (8)
19 See 27
23 Fast but not flimsy underwear, the breath of earth (5,5)
24 Hot spot taken from earth to Venus (4)
26 Another name for Giuglio? Go away! (5)
27,19 Lancaster's bad, bad habits keep nothing from prophets of war (9,6)
28 Algerian liberator with copper for plate in the Hebrides (9)
29 You heard bad news? Remove stitches (5)

DOWN

1,2 Such trees 16 enrage relation (7-7)
3 See 5
4 Plump for constant partner (6)
5,3 Meadows superior and hot in mysterious poem 16 (8-4)
6 The man from Porlock changed terrain to mountain (10)
7 Composer (original name) no good for Keats' charities when 1ac (7)
8 OT prophet beheaded, taking gold from alchemist's heater (7)
13 Such war is total, as Antonio's bosom was exposed (2,3,5)
16 Starting place of poem sees Greek king turning up in endless river (2,6)
17 Obese and uncouth fellow has Domino maybe to throw (3,4)
18 Sporting building topped in island valley (7)
20 Setting of 10, not measurable, cold, with turn out of hell (7)
21 Excellent thing Cordelia did at twilight (7)
22 Inability to bear all that one can imagine accepting initially (6)
25 Elder brother in Bible and thesaurus (4)

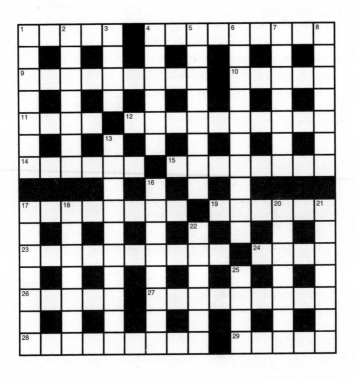

Macbeth was compared to 24 14, who would '——' (2 to be unruffled as White Teeth's author) (3,4,3,5,3,3,3,4). The solution to this, which is not itself a quotation from the play, is to go around the perimeter of the diagram clockwise, beginning *at the bottom left-hand corner*. Remaining solutions are to be fitted into the diagram jigsaw-wise, wherever they will go.

1   Sticker for lady in a depression (8)
2   Assistance keeping river dry (4)
3   Song from 'The Gondoliers' (one in endless grain) (10)
4   Mechanical base (6)
5   Slope has both ends of Barchester on a drug (4)
6   Dunderhead's method of sailing boat (4)
7   Poet wins first part of race in the orient (8)
8   Puzzle with variations (6)
9   The truth is, diamonds are a substitute for rubber (7)
10 A lot of country, a lot of frost, the sailors cry (5-3)
11 Setter's on front page with soldiers (4)
12 Cheese comes in below, like … (2,5)
13 … what Mr Micawber said, more than half-inched? (2,5)
14 See 24
15 Working dog? (See 'The Pursuit of Love') (8)
16 Like Mrs Gummidge from A Christmas Carol or Nicholas Nickleby (4)
17 An artefact is nearly nymphomaniac (3,3)
18 Underground worker concealing fear from psychologist? (4-6)
19 Poet of love and ruin (4)
20 When I say nothing, it's active service for you, my lads (2,8)
21 Painter copied a lot (4)
22 Bespectacled student in desire after oxygen (6)
23 Have been captured by the enemy – captured by guide that used to run the railways (5,5)
24,14 Italian river, killer colour, with principal time for proverbial pet (3,4,3,2,3,5)
25 Alternatively I promise to sound (read differently) singularly like Carreras Domingo and Pavarotti (10)
26 Bone of a beautiful nature (4)
27 Ecru is clue Ben had changed (10)
28 'Bear with me' (staff of castle, fighting fire-raiser) (7)

ACROSS

1   Gay Gordon's finale after Catullus's girl (7)
5   Prepared for destruction by God, repeatedly so without direction (4,3)
9   Leaves to save trouble about pet (7)
10 Director's friend at last (7)
11 The Reverend Mr Jenkins of the Liberal Party (3)
12 Singing along with small object for drunk Irishman? (7)
13 Senior churchman losing head over flower girl is rarely boring (7)
14 See 19
19,14 Maybe metaphysical aroma surrounding regular teeth with new filling upset your pet (11,7,4)
24 19 14 was cricket captain (7)
26 King of France keeps ship, home to composer (7)
27 Bird of English and Greek character (3)
28 Original good start to reference book of which are many matters (7)
29 19 14, more than a wonder (7)
30 19 14, object of Ada Clare's love (7)
31 19 14, as above with different boy (7)

DOWN

1   19 14 with a penchant for crochet? (8)
2   19 14 not yet weaned (8)
3   Arouses interest in dress in a day (9)
4   On the contrary, say about … say, flowers (7)
5   Staggering – so am I – of gangster (7)
6   19 14 talk finished (5)
7   19 14 doing short distance at great speed (6)
8   19 14, little room with little damp (6)
15 Later laureate sounding easy (3)
16 Person with money put foot down endlessly and comparatively safely (9)
17 Aboriginal's first to use spade in river (8)
18 Little connection with a lot of missives that trade on superstition (8)
20 Painter and soldier during holiday with king (3,4)
21 Drink rum, a habit partial to which is an African liberator (7)

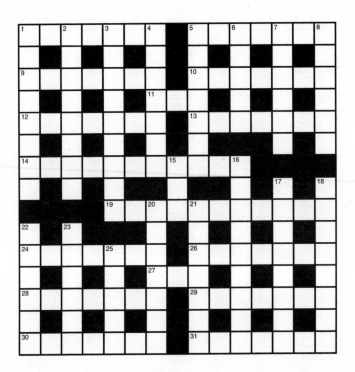

22 Certify 1 and 5 with painful sound (6)
23 Criminal crocodile (6)
25 Female's first language? (5)

Across solutions include five pairs from the same play whose clues are partial.

ACROSS

 1 Girl's goal reversed (6)
 4 MS with Pa replaced by Ma (other way, other place) (7)
 8 Can —— the bellows-mender? (6)
 9 On 4 across's head be it, like snow in front of sledge (4,4)
 11 Fruit coming out to play (9)
 12 Fruit to admit defeat (5)
 13 Fruit of 11 with two replacements compassed by bending sickle (4,3)
 14 East for spider, not North, which is a pain (7)
 17 Love's is one, it's said: snags do develop (3,4)
 18 Tis? (periodically 22s?) (7)
 20 Leading such as 9 (5)
 23 Mitre turned into God? (9)
 24 Foundation about which it's wrong to rely (8)
 25 Award for small boy (6)
 26 California and Arizona? (7)
 27 This is Montana (6)

DOWN

 1 Aggie the egg-breaker? (7)
 2 Dire poems sadly enforced again (9)
 3 Confused situation with Araucaria's relative the tailless dormouse having nothing (9)
 4 Appreciation of theatre during ceremony to go with correspondence (7,5)
 5 It isn't safe to assume teaching of religion will get you to heaven (5)
 6 Low points for beast (5)
 7 Big wet mark made by childless masons? (7)
 10 Nature deity inverted in 23's waking call to 27 (5,7)
 15 Having revolutionary capacity to destroy a piece of furniture (9)
 16 Warden having organized recce, go in (9)
 17 Try about everything vegetable (7)
 19 Golden girl of classical Italy (7)
 21 Top men with girl to follow (5)
 22 Movement coming in to have Ramadan celebrated (5)

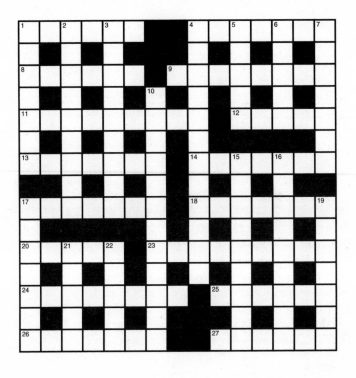

ACROSS

(Solutions to the following italicised clues do not appear in the puzzle; they are given to fill in the gaps in the quotation.)

A condition of the title is that

1 'He refuses to hope, sadly: they demanded bows ... (3,5,2,5)
   ... Intelligence for the Pope on previous situations ... (9,3)

11 ... Member is inland at four, isn't it? ... (11,4)
   ... D in A (as in AD) highly commended by Mischief's repair on books ... (3,5,9,2,3)

21 ... It has to put in 'feature' (replacing 'feet err') ... (4,2,9)
   ... With yacht the miners wrecked ... (2,7,5,4)

25 ... Stand over prohibition (2,3,10)' (Author mentioned below)

9 Eyot has a tenant (5)

10 A little sugar in place of beer? (9)

12 Ship's engineer, like when Germaine's about (7)

14 Sonny swallowed drug in Suffolk town (7)

16 Shakespeare's doctor in Trollope's Last Chronicle (7)

19 Poet with subject of ballad to the Queen (7)

23 Move money – good to see responsible use of it (9)

24 The two to one in former South African politics (5)

DOWN

1 Top-heavy seen from behind? (4,5)

2 Virgil's point, signal to start about diary (7)

3 Polar hero or conspirator talking of food (5)

4 Blonde given hair-do when pressure is high? (3,4)

5 Bairnsfather's ex-beak in the police (3,4)

6 Emetic required after vegetable when it's piping? (9)

7 Quotation from former pamphlet? (7)

8 Piece dropped around river (5)

13 Confection with courses the wrong way round (9)

15 Am insured for change of carer (9)

17 Property of beadle and academic, whence the great conqueror (7)

18 West Indian father first leaving Searle's saint (7)

19 'In short, when I've a smattering of elemental strategy, you'll say a better Major General has never ——' (Gilbert) (3,1,3)

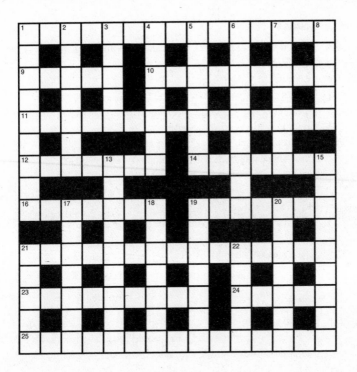

20 Ranges of colour for painting fungi the other way (7)
21 'I'd toddle safely home and die ——' (Sassoon) (with the flowers?) (2,3)
22 Meaningful picture created by Rankin (5)

ACROSS

9   Ian and Colin in place of Compo, Clegg and Foggy (9)

10 A window in Oxford (5)

11 Coconut for Constable (5)

12 Naughty Katie won't start to pull (4,2,3)

13 Opening in metal will be annoying without check on house (5,4)

14 Channel bird at end of journey (5)

15 Country (Nicaragua) wanting peace (7)

17 Time bird came back for Mothering Sunday (7)

19 Shy boy – who's he? (5)

21 It's advisable for former partner to get put in prison when about to leave the world (9)

23 Day Clarke broadcast contraindicated for slimmers (5-4)

24 Love and be an appetiser (5)

25 A measure of corn helps to give Joseph a hand (5)

26 Reduction comes when psychiatry is prevalent? (9)

DOWN

1,5,3,6,8   The dog said not many gave information to the king and his mistress about split with Doris: noted bass in article audible to the audience injures humble characters from ear to heel (3,6,6,3,5,2,7, 3,3,6,4,5,6,3,3,3)

2   Mistake about woolly (8)

3   See 1

4   It's good to take rubbish to the cave (6)

5   See 1

6   See 1

7   Ancient weapon (6)

8   See 1

16 Opening for foolish parson in church (8)

18 Heard of a jolly old prison across the water (8)

20 Law-giving potato (6)

22 It's my mistake in Jim (say), the French boy (6)

ACROSS

9   A French hundred dollar version of The Lucky Fugitive (4,5)
10 Pole to copy ancient Egyptian monarch (5)
11 See 1
12 Operatic lady with rival and one other (5,6)
13 Jonson's small boy's revolutionary haze (9)
15 King in iron, a king of sport (5)
16 Irreligious way to prepare dinner? (7)
17 Qualify one to pursue hospital department outlet (7)
18 Don't talk quietly's a complaint (5)
19 Hamlet's friend makes a little room turn into a planet (9)
20 Cobbett's London retreat for wrestling is Walden's neighbour (7,4)
21 The snare of alcohol (3)
22 Straight man in charge? (5)
23 Don't talk about Tangly Dell seen without bulbs (6-3)

DOWN

1,3,11,6,8,2 (The) Piers, with sea bird in pile quiet, left strange journalist at hospital: I profanely utter a song of Sinatra that's beheaded and died: Fox takes ship to headland with little Andrew about to finish fixing painter (7,8,7,3,5,3,3,4,3,5,2,8,3,2,4)
2   See 1
3   See 1
4   Survey heaven in metres (8)
5   Whole milk skimmed for disheartened cat (6)
6   See 1
7   One in three chance of being flat is not meant (10)
8   See 1
14 Cautious about China student with attractive style (10)
17 Overture keeps engineers in Cumbria (8)
19 Conductor (as cited in Patience) of Comus first arranged (6)
21 First for actor Hermione after 21ac (4)

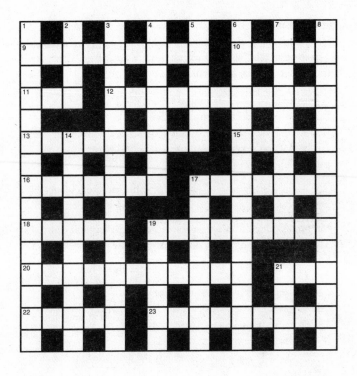

His fond question was 4 7 11: the answer is the perimeter read clockwise *from the bottom right-hand corner* plus 26 (4,4,5,3,4,4,5,3,4). Remaining solutions are to go in the diagram jigsaw-wise, wherever they will go. Clues are listed in alphabetical order of their solutions.

   1 A Turner (The Unlikely Lad) – he has done many pictures (4,4)

   2 A painter enlarged a departed leader (6)

   3 Reportedly purchase love, swallowing second tooth (8)

4,7,11 Go bald when retired, about precise period in time (see preamble) (4,3,5,3,6)

   5 Dreadful failure, I leave, getting severe criticism (6)

   6 Dangerous disease renders ours viable (5,5)

   7 See 4

   8 Minute structure in heart problem – lie right left and centre first (6)

   9 The fellow's a nonsense, coming upon a body in the summer (4,4)

  10 Small residence for American chopper on April 1st? (4)

  11 See 4

  12 Lake with a friend in a part of it (6)

  13 Idle around on bridgehead on the Eden (said Bondman George) (7)

  14 1/1 river comes in close (3,4)

  15 Momentary piece of intestinal folds (6)

  16 Greek characters are funny losing head with some snores when returning (8)

  17 Five shillings possess about half the cemetery (3,5)

  18 Ring loses brightness at church to look like mother-of-pearl (8)

  19 Do – moved with virtue – hit your tee shot further (8)

  20 Excursion from closet? (6)

  21 List of duties to entertain love bird (7)

  22 FC with Diamonds loses them, like mats of old from Moscow, say (6)

  23 Issue simple command from Ryde – so what? (3,3,4)

  24 Sailor with ethical tautology? (6)

  25 Speedwell for saint with handkerchief (first missing from nave and choir) (8)

  26 Christmas vocalist first in intelligence (4)

  27 Having crashed our motor torpedo boat we are left with a twisted shell (4,4)

  28 Huntsmen dressed in greasy woollens, they say (6)

According to Wilde's Mrs Allonby, when good Americans they die go to Paris. The shaded squares in the grid show that 'the Smith of Smiths' (though without reference to Americans) had the idea first. (5,2, [merely] 2,12,2,8). Remaining solutions are to go in the diagram jigsaw-wise, wherever they will go. Clues are listed in alphabetical order of their solutions.

1 Chiltern town in royal shire where pet lost tail and died (11)
2 Polishes 'The Regiment' (5)
3 Disastrous place for the aristocrat in Miss Campbell (9)
4 Special cord in soiled container to deprive of possession (11)
5 Ruler to act threatening to have your head chopped off (9)
6 Most foolish man ultimately to accept honour (7)
7 The genie to form a majority? (8)
8 'Double Thickness' played by Donald Wolfit (4,2,3)
9 Keep hot and cold without direction (6)
10 African periodical turned some Italian white (7)
11 Hot and cold area reversal needs a lot of cracking (4,3)
12 Raise one into a large number (5)
13 Example of batting posture (8)
14 Races in appearance with no fingers (6)
15 Shearer's doctor's for change of air (5)
16 What a pity the poem is audible to the listener! (2,4)
17 Made an approach quickly put together (3,2)
18 Recover memory of Italian king with English king's name (7)
19 Was generous again when retired (9)
20 Cricket score for keeping chickens (3)
21 Girl of riches and rags (6)
22 Fast driver taking drug has troubled rest (9)
23 Mooring place for converted atheist (7)
24 Totnes's wrongly placed on the Great Ouse (2,5)
25 Some corruption it's not (5)
26 Time for colleague to agree (5)
27 Doll makes a drop on the page (9)
28 M Chopin's address to his amie (8)
29 Preceding period shortly exhibited by Paul Taylor (3)
30 Top coat or new top, no match for lion (7)
31 Green food is the tops (8)
32 Drunk in a brew? This is perhaps the wrong place (4,3)

ACROSS

1 Music shop keeper has where to put his catch (6)
4,10,9,31 Excessive use of sharpener discouraged by 28 (3,2,3,3,4,1,5,4,2)
12,19 I would follow one with a sound speed, said 25 18dn (Jeremiah said it first) (1,2,1,5)
13,29,22 What 1ac would hardly stand is inimitable impudence (10,4,2,10)
15 20's demand for fish meunière (starters) in special case (5,2,2)
18 Troilus's father's relations with public sector of 12 (5)
19 See 12
20 Grandfather's minor problem for gardener (9)
22 See 13
25,18dn Harold to take the cream from leading position (8)
28 Law stationer with problems at hand (7)
29 See 13
30 Worth a visit to the theatre? (8)
31 See 4

DOWN

1 Second to last in permanent way? Nuts (7)
2 Get oneself ready to be married? (5)
3 Bird of prey makes boy lose way (4)
5 Eye – choose one and see what you hear (5)
6 Unsatisfactory model put up to scouts (5)
7 There's a margin in mine; Araucaria's unsophisticated (9)
8 Draw light from roof structure (3,4)
11 Various people taking the plunge (6)
14 See 27
16 Insouciant retort from a hundred fairies (2,2,1,4)
17 Dramatist with moderate horse (6)
18 See 25
19 Wakes up to love after a lot of food (5,2)
21 Having maximum humidity is a barrier to the plague (7)
23 Much of 30 from Ascot (5)
24 Left idly composing a poem (5)
26 King on a river nearly finds scene of massacre (5)
27,14 Some elephants appeal for a starter (4,4)

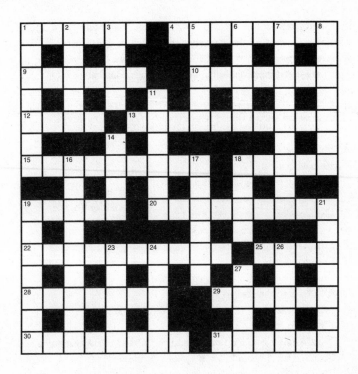

The perimeter, read across the top, down the right hand side, down the left, and across the bottom, is Capulet's lament to his cousin at their feast (3,3,1,3,4,3,7,4). Remaining solutions are to go in the diagram jigsaw-wise, wherever they will go. Clues are listed in alphabetical order of their solutions.

1 Call to prayer from railway in Forfarshire (7)
2 A piratical vicar's friend restraining hot offbeat nature (10)
3 Tea is available from ferryman (6)
4 Shy objects in firms given to folly (8)
5 Fish with a tail (4)
6 Harmony as opposed to binding (7)
7 Scrubber of space station in the ocean (7)
8 Goddess of poetry has come for a joker (4)
9 Twin servants take number from disc, one of exceptional size (7)
10 Good – jolly good – last year's leaders, so as to be unputdownable? (10)
11 Post supporters for Milan team's cup match (8)
12 Old foot soldier called Jerome (4)
13 Opportunity for praying mantis, possibly (6)
14 One who steals pounds (6)
15 Not belonging to a union, to sum up Thatcher's aphorism? (3-7)
16 Seller of apples is a killer, a violent criminal (10)
17 Tennyson's girl has much 19th century bric-a-brac (6)
18 Bowling (slow) with too much doctoring? (8)
19 Have risen from my bed, going back (being a cat) (4)
20 Bring up what was cut off the high priest's servant (Luke) (4)
21 Smelling of payment without benefit (8)
22 Composer helps to give the squire's pig his dinner (8)
23 Musical sewer? (6)
24 Garden pest without formality tucked into water regulator (10)
25 S-Sunday in Lent could cause breathlessness (10)
26 One meal like another topped and tailed like 7 (8)
27 Posh dads are poison (4)
28 Girl finds 5 in a river of Burgundy (6)

Perimeter, clockwise* *from the dotted square*: Ideas about Greek legend (beginners 0-4) – chaotic battles about Dodona building – are 22 according to 23 (3,7,2,3,5,3,5). Remaining solutions are to go in the diagram jigsaw-wise, wherever they will go. Clues are listed in alphabetical order of their solutions.

1   Boy or girl in the American dream (6)
2   Second and first rib, say (4)
3   Mushroom takes light container for squid (10)
4   A great number – over 9 in centigrammes – is degrading (10)
5   Middle name of President Mandela unmanned by refusal (6)
6   Dries up fibre into even letters to depress (8)
7   Smoother mood doesn't start grasping a prey that wriggles (5,5)
8   Francs keeping German provinces in Belgium (8)
9   Treading liquid on slope (8)
10 Get ready to start spring in pub (6)
11 Canal builder has reduced letters (7)
12 Pester to get rule (not English) back in Ulster (6)
13 Car for my French and Latin god (6)
14 Fungal growth from the lake or a whirl (3,7)
15 German river with Australian backing for town near Treviso (6)
16 Formerly not repeated unless … (4)
17 … repeated over again (4,4)
18 Get back, say, in the wet (6)
19 Check reportedly expensive present transporters (8)
20 Start again in the belfry to remove from the statute book (6)
21 Revival of musical with Dickensian character (4)
22 Group doing performances without publicity (7)
23 Novel poet (7)
24 Kind of circus or theatre (4)
25 Wrong, badly, with a Spanish omelette (8)
26 Relative at Northchurch to open out fingers? (8)
27 Get us a page turner to put in the shade (7)
28 Fighter to put twists into the road (8)

* Because the grid is wholly symmetrical, it will work just as well if the perimeter runs anticlockwise: it won't read so well, but if you have filled it in this way don't feel you have to rub it all out and start again.

ACROSS

1 Disappointment for 27's appeal to mountaineer (8)
5 Some shine at place for Keats's peonies (6)
9 Crazy car takes specialist publisher to arboretum (8)
10 6's car (6)
11 Killer coming in to be devil-buster (8)
12 Top man in ball (6)
14 Queen's follower on the ground or the railway? (5,5)
18 Male people with no 2 (10)
22 6's colours for the ears (6)
23 Commemoration of wisecrack about presiding deity (8)
24 6 like Oliver Cromwell's face? (6)
25 6 taking fish to water (8)
26 6's uninteresting study (6)
27 6 heard enquiring if Wimbledon's being broadcast (8)

DOWN

1 6 could be Crabbe, taking one for one (6)
2 6's proposal (6)
3 Winner getting fed up with spoil (6)
4 6 with his medium, desert (10)
6 One crowned with gold plate? (8)
7 6 to live with jet set on island (8)
8 Struggle with bells? (4-4)
13 Crown reportedly keeps bill for tinned food (10)
15 Gave up to use teeth during scattering of seed (8)
16 Grey-haired emblem on railway (8)
17 Worker to run away with jumper (8)
19 6 raised little girl then little boy (6)
20 Time off in space (6)
21 Without upward look the gun will be nicked (6)

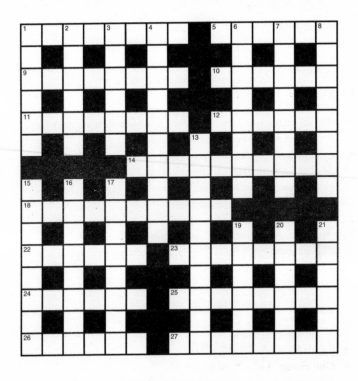

Associated in Parliament with 15 are: Sir 1 24, Sir 8 7, Sir 18 17, Mr 4, Mr 6, Mr 23 and Mr 22 down. These may have partial clues.

ACROSS

7 Drink and cause collision (7)
8 Note about 'Bloody' (7)
10 Bloody prime minister holds back punishment for striker (10)
11 Primate keeping second part of church (4)
12 I got passed over endlessly – fancy! (4)
13 Topped non-medical bed from abroad first referring to services (10)
15 Novel hero, if sane, moving between pubs (7,4)
19 Gentle wish resolved horizontally (10)
20 The Christmas cheat? (4)
21 'Half way down the stairs' would it be? (1,3)
22 International body in lodging nearly perished due to old volcano (5,5)
23 Turn to hill in time (7)
24 One who owes, owes (7)

DOWN

1 Shakespearean lover (7)
2 Girl with a gun has docked (6)
3 Undressed food was a shocker (5,5)
4 Mr Mandelson leaves the de Winter house (4)
5 Rainstorm near the Taj Mahal affecting the land (8)
6 Lawman (7)
9 Inconstant as of old, new car is on tour (11)
14 Clergy keeping spirit up with cat's-eyes (10)
16 Called 'love' by rider's abstraction (4,4)
17 Spelling competitions are on the increase (7)
18 It turns a fairy on its tail (7)
20 Depression our hue? (6)
22 £1000 a day? (4)

In the W 23 6 Apollo says '5 is 4dn; 3 7; 18dn 24 1dn; 26 a 27 13; etc.' Clues to these solutions may be partial.

ACROSS

1 Pointed instrument indicated with hash key (5)
4 Old king keeps men in the same place that can stick together (9)
9 Sheepish remark about little stream for seaside plant (7)
10 Come to after snooze while discussing a post-mortem affair? (7)
11 Queen's favourite to be 10? (5)
12 Banality of 1 and 10 in lock (9)
13 Not a single return in the races (6)
15 Scene 1 could be always remembered (4,4)
18 Call to East German 'a time to keep cool' (8)
19 Pieces played by spouse (6)
22 Cross point off: princess's head's in jewelled piece – she's not one for an only child (9)
24,1dn What an authentic verb must have? (1,4,7)
26 Reported corollary of Stockton on Solent? (7)
27 In France I have a name? Not I (7)
28 Tell a senior NCO to put his butt on the ground (5,4)
29 Key to action when there's a lot of fever (5)

DOWN

1 See 24
2 French town lethally concealing a potential father-in-law (5)
3 Bohemian (9)
4 Pursued by reporter (6)
5 Recluse endlessly single (8)
6 Old as Don Pedro called Hero (5)
7 Aaaaah! (Halt within) (9)
8 Writer chap keeps me and loses his head (7)
14 A do with a lorry in trouble on the king's highway? (5,4)
16 Otherwise see about arrangement for publicity for the prom (9)
17 Master idiot in vehicle needing oil (8)
18 Firm retaining a place for manufacturing (7)
20 Poet with opening of sonnet is writing to his sovereign (7)

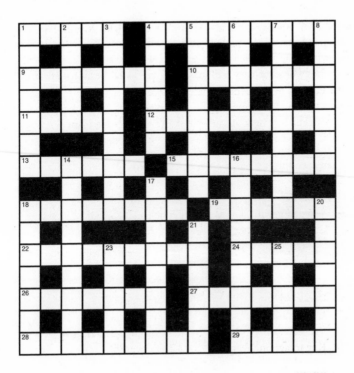

21 Pilgrims who invert their struggles? (6)
23 Avail oneself of spadework (5)
25 Nonsense about the very large that can be ruled (5)

In the shaded squares (read always from left to right) are to be placed (with some repetition) 'Three women with cowslip plants (one sheet) make a bed at bedtime' (3,6,3,7,5,3,3,5). Remaining solutions are to go in the diagram jigsaw-wise, wherever they will go. Clues are listed in alphabetical order of their solutions.

1   It isn't there to which the sailor was posted (6)
2   Bill Fox held loud shot to be an accident (3,2,3)
3   It is blown up by accident (6)
4   In the morning put cheeses in cupboards (7)
5   Records of old Indian and some old British money (6)
6   Fruit I can arrange to be put in ... say the fridge? (9)
7   I leave city with saint in it, which helps (7)
8   Article about Cancer, maybe unfinished, by Belladonna? (7)
9   Report of one who kidnaps a dictator ... (6)
10   ... whose troops are for hospital or in beds ... (7)
11   ... with Rubicon almost crossed, according to Athenian judge (6)
12   Baby food one follows in cars (7)
13   Study play with king's name (5)
14   Student holds one that was forbidden (5)
15   Writer returns on time, taking on a bit of kidney (7)
16   Catcher (anon) turning East (5)
17   Takes no account of beauty that is past? (9)
18   Using pure oils is risky (8)
19   Will help to change resort (8)
20   Battle of modern girl among artists (9)
21   Authority is dumb (3-2)
22   Female beast takes on cabinet maker (8)
23   Quicker (-tempered?) at card game by the seaside? (8)
24   One holding weapon which is found in Scots river (8)
25   Collector with point on pen cut short, about to wander up (8)
26   Our author rhymes with meat (8)
27   Disarrange form of solute (6)
28   Don't rely on what is said in conveyance (5,4)
29   Peninsula whence came the Limerick lady with a 25 (6)
30   Not stable – it may be thrown (6)

The perimeter clockwise from the top left-hand corner is the first line of a poem which could be dated 20th January 1820. Remaining solutions must be entered in the diagram jigsaw-wise, wherever they will fit in; their clues are listed in alphabetical order of the solutions.

1   I leave counters for a nomogram (4)
2   With the fourth part of play it's always the second part of speech that performs (6,4)
3   Put off a right to possess a 10 incompletely (8)
4   Biggest drop in the world, that's Lucifer's (5,5)
5   At a distance of about three feet? (4,6)
6   Don makes the most of article about five ounces (4)
7   Eric is Keith's centre-half in the homeland (6)
8   Swift move with instruments (4)
9   Performed without mistake by a deconstructionist (7)
10   Diplomatic record approved on Tyneside (8)
11   Strip the rich man of his shirt? (6)
12   Risk loss of cool after goal (8)
13   Appearance of devotion without assent is always a bad thing (3-7)
14   One possibly green in conclusion, maybe a goddess (4,6)
15   Leave coat on water (8)
16   Pip's Joe missing a place for cars and one for trains (7)
17   Setter's a journalist and has been making his mark (10)
18   Director of silent films to turn before long to talkies? (8)
19   Cover for love in Venice? (4)
20   Girl first with the Fates (6)
21   Nearly but not quite dark? (4)
22   Man of mark outside church, far from the day of the perimeter (8)
23   Cover for films (6)
24   Scattered, I believe, between poles (6)
25   Estate building in China? (3,3)
26   Time to cause a stir with underground food (7)
27   Merchant's name in the season of the perimeter, according to Mr Weller (7)
28   A little bit of Sunday (4)

The perimeter suggests liquor and bad language: bush worse, wine worse? a bit worse, I suspect (1,5,3,3,1,5,4,1,5). Remaining solutions are to go in the diagram jigsaw-wise, wherever they will go. Clues are listed in alphabetical order of their solutions.

1 Parts of insect for one that has any audible? (8)
2 Tall chap to live at an advantageous position (8)
3 Lover finds romance with turn to Montagu's place (8)
4 Clue would require 'O for a Frankish king!' (6)
5 The Spanish speaker heard to amuse is dubious (10)
6 Politician in country that got out of this (6)
7 Healthy sign preceding 'Sweet chariot' (4)
8 Mansion for prophet with you (say) instead of me, praise the Lord! (10)
9 Dour doctor breaking rule swallowed by fish (10)
10 Stun gun following devil's attack (6)
11 End clueing? Could be a pleasure! (10)
12 Little time for the German bodyguard (6)
13 Little anything for the condominium (4)
14 Little time rating for old people (4)
15 Old priest topped in part of church with guns in 1961 film (8)
16 Rectangular Russian flower (see National Guard) (6)
17 Nothing wrong about the article – it will be all right … (2,3,5)
18 Nice characters in return for skilled (10)
19 Spring harvest takes heart from minister (4)
20 Almost regretting first word of Gray's curse (4)
21 Raphael's holy uncle? (6)
22 Certify with your name or a cross? (4)
23 Infection caused by bad housing and drug (4)
24 Arch-destroyer put in drink the wrong way for it to go down (7)
25 Old trust in bridge for county town (4)
26 Providing Ben with culture will give you a bumpy ride (10)
27 Regulation overturned and lamp broken in plan for pin-up (4,3)
28 Little pin roughly cut from tree (7,3)

ACROSS

 1 First person's frog, second person's man (6)
 4 Throws me out of Hampshire – my place was in Shropshire (8)
10 Go quietly, accepting failure in Derbyshire (7)
11 See 9
12 Callers 'like mastodons bellowing across primeval swamps' (5)
13 Unstraightforward direction – lion loose in the neighbourhood (3-6)
14 Bookie's way to incite small boy (8)
16 Mrs 26, best of 12, out of the bed for the winter (6)
18 Little fellow from Northants (6)
20 Mr 26, no civil rights activist, the pawnbroker's cat (5,3)
24 I'm taking the service away: I'm unable to keep one (9)
25 Little Rosie M, retaining flowers (5)
26 Farceur's time with party-goers (7)
27 Lack of enthusiasm for love in a monkey (7)
28 10 was seated on a pile of hay (8)
29 Miss Wickham has lost a policeman (6)

DOWN

 1 Just half the transmitters show the Prince of Wales (3-4)
 2 Articulate your part – there must be no uncertainty (7)
 3 Female endings for letters (5)
 5 It's great about Honduras taking water from Bangladesh (6)
 6 'Hear me ——' (psalm or hymn) – female in charge in financial
    street (4,1,4)
 7 Bertrand's sound sound (7)
 8 Miss 10's house number raising the wind (7)
9,11 Mrs, worst of 12, old sailor with some work regulations
    continuing (7,7)
15 Leave revolutionary in European river with bonhomie (4,5)
17 A drink about to cook for 25dn and 26 (7)
18 'We ——s do not lightly forget', so wrote author (7)
19 Dish in antiquity with faint horns (7)
21 Monastic emblem carrying weight no doubt (7)

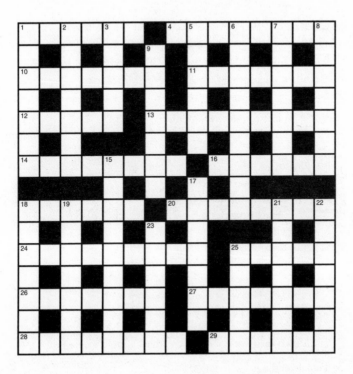

22 Beast with vital something keeps capsized ship backed by 25dn for
    the 1:30 at Lewes (4-3)

23 Analyse a hundred and three or so light years (6)

25 Little place for rubbish to be put (5)

Perimeter, clockwise *from the dotted square*: After 'the 26 and the 23 8', exeunt leaders (3,8,3,3,5,6). Remaining solutions are to go in the diagram jigsaw-wise, wherever they will go. Clues are listed in alphabetical order of their solutions.

1 Embarrassed one that was victim of strike (7)
2 A disease I discovered in rodent (6)
3 Those who take things to pieces without some sadism get huntsmen's trophies (7)
4 Blacking of old for a beast in a shelter (8)
5 Hot days for young chickens (8)
6 Nothing in beast but fur? (4)
7 Dickens's Rosa provides missile for the French (6)
8 Roman period comes to an end (4)
9 Tropical flier finds doctor ready for off (6)
10 Drug subsequently fashionable as purgative (8)
11 Currency company used forgery (6)
12 Man and boy first wept for by player in play (6)
13 Desire for cobbler's symbol eventually is at it (4,4)
14 Protestant in the lunar eclipse (8)
15 One's own turn for standard type that's caught inside (5,5)
16 Drink by agreement (6)
17 Game with central hole? (4)
18 Captive with quilt – I sound off – makes readily disintegrating plumage (6,4)
19 Type of rock with wordplay at its end (4)
20 Sharpener of musical monologue about Robin-Hood style movie hero holding saint (5-5)
21 Confidential article on hormones, for example (7)
22 Film studio found by entering town with mallet, say (10)
23 Making a noise about little university ghost (8)
24 Measurer causing a stir – and maybe a storm? (8)
25 Fighter with newspaper —— to wrap his fish and chips? (8)
26 Trouble inside last month (6)
27 Sound of passing fliers who love silence? (6)
28 Last lot of fliers left first by protestant (7)

ACROSS

8 In Britain, in France, Queen's definitely not so hot (5)

9 He had left far off 'dim drums throbbing, in the hills ———'
(Chesterton) (4,5)

11 Climber with a fast entry to the saint of love (9)

12 Two circles on the drums (5)

13 Insect and vegetable nearly provide father to … (7)

14 … mythological changer of form and posture (7)

15 11 and 14 who met 10 let little general out (3,3,9)

18 Defence of good wine being swallowed (7)

21 Reported place for crossword compiler as maid to … (7)

23 … the nameless apostate (5)

24 Thicket found by fellow where river enters sea (9)

25 Start to grow white fur – unfinished – in entry (9)

26 11's man, more dopey than swift? (5)

DOWN

1 11's girl: who's she? (6)

2 Charlotte Bronte's little town (8)

3 Refuse to turn up absolutely fresh (5-3)

4 Cooked hog – carrion – accompanying elements of church
music (5,5)

5 Happy song (4)

6 Day 10, perhaps, was after 1 (6)

7 14's man's old weapon (6)

10 Calls to abandon wrongdoing (5,2)

14 Page 50 means trouble for broadcast contests (5,5)

15 Vessel portraying man and dog at prison (4,3)

16 Where the French sit their father at their final destination (8)

17 Things for personnel are dull at the lakes (8)

19 Talk about home guard's payment (6)

20 Sloping out of Verona etc (6)

22 Refer to everything potentially due (6)

24 Seafood or apple for 7's hard-hearted dog (4)

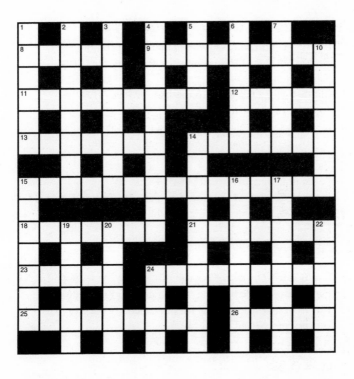

The perimeter (3,6,5,2,7,2,3) contains the author's name; it has an R in it. The line before the perimeter contains both parts of the title, early 28, 19 and God, and finishes with 23.

1 City where a lot of mozzarella is made? (6)
2 Gold adds flavour to patronage (8)
3 City operations transcribed by transcriber (7)
4 Sin – enter hell, coming to dust? (6)
5 City retreat a treat to eat (6)
6 Pick small boy in charge of such mail (10)
7 Assist in getting introduction to the wife (8)
8 In which to go for a jaunt with flower girl and arch-forger? (5,3)
9 Many inches to the mile found on big fish (5-5)
10 Ultimate layabout (4)
11 Mummy turns to anticolonial movement (3,3)
12 Body reached by remote control (6)
13 Griefs caused by motorway run (8)
14 Fantastic comrade first and foster-father to Esther (8)
15 City in France like on a hill for parliamentary pioneer (5,5)
16 City in France liked by all? (4)
17 Related to vision? You must be oking (6)
18 People who braid their hair sound like dishes (8)
19 Most of the newspapers reporting you to me are taking liberties (7)
20 Malay boat with deserter still in it is in proportion (3,4)
21 Counsel for Frederick Forsyth (4)
22 Relative I abandoned – which I greatly enjoyed (8)
23 Examination of feet etc? (4)
24 Composer, a Trojan, leaving – he's met an actor (7)
25 Severe weather warning for mortals worried over member (5,5)
26 Second vehicle came out (6)
27 Bird at Christmas with no first name (6)
28 Solver, surely, of puzzle (8)

55 Riders in the Ocean

ACROSS

8 Ungulate of ungulate, tailless in March or September (7)

9 Rig a triangle of short grass? (7)

10 See 14

11 Where they grow successions of things going back to back (9)

13 See 14

14,22,10,3,13 A swinger wearing dark glasses is the Protestant free-trader, one up on the 18ac in a 25 19 (in Bramley's carol), at pub without consent close to time – that's one of 9ac's 9dn (2,5,2, 6,3,6,6,4,6,5,2,1,5,5)

18 Outstanding people put sailor where he should be … (5)

20 … eclipsed by grass amid ruinous ruins (6,3)

22 See 14

24 Cornish flower with French spirit once dominant in Spain (7)

25 Cool off? (7)

DOWN

1 Irishman at Northchurch, Sir Walter Elliot's Hall (8)

2 Fairy Queen's wrinkle (6)

3 See 14

4 Student under the chopper has German name (4)

5 Acrylic fibre with no fat coming up (6)

6 Searched untidily for a drink before wise man died (8)

7 Speculate about fool of a dog (6)

9 Cup of Pym's – Crosby's doesn't hold so much (9)

12 I can nurse to provide cover (9)

15 Greeting in rowing centre (not English) like 18ac (8)

16 Diana was savage over hair (8)

17 Holiness caught within reason (8)

18 Begin to be contrasted (3,3)

19 What 18ac do is about right in a holy place (6)

21 Outstanding indication (6)

23 Little boy going down the plughole? (4)

Solutions to asterisked clues are 15's man's men; their further definitions, if any, may be derived from the text of the play.

ACROSS

- *1 Bloody boy within was fine (7)
- *5 Banter holding letter (6)
- *10 Article taken from paint stripper (8)
- *11 It's a dog (6)
- 13 Throw things and hide (4)
- 14 Hard year for the town by the marsh (5)
- 15 3 17 (4)
- *18 Unorthodox Athenian student with unfinished coat (9)
- 20 Dangerous as Esau (5)
- 22 Set to mature pointlessly (5)
- 23 Tool put into effect (9)
- *25 One doing the same for Orlando was fine (4)
- *27 Flag uncoloured overhead (5)
- 29,30 Mine's ill prepared for discouraging obesity (8)
- *32 Good drink for 10 (6)
- *33 Saint for Christmas that's shortened in prison (8)
- *34,*35 Those deficient in weaponry and footwear in Archers of old (6,7)

DOWN

- 2 Dancing 3 to toe in opera (9)
- 3 Virgin soldier has both hands (4)
- 4 Recruit for the wood in Macbeth (5)
- 6 Does nothing matter but music? (4)
- 7 Minor player taking part of Sir Oliver Martext ran away (5)
- 8 Why pointlessly cover willow with knitwear? (7)
- 9 Tree and woodland deity under fire (3-3)
- *12 Two characters in King John sound stimulating (6)
- *16 River, sacred one, was fine (5)
- 17 Demonstrate about right to insecticide (5)
- 19 Setter's about to stay put (6)
- 21 Correction for Eulalie left in turn-out – it must go first (1,4,1,3)
- 22 Good girl's detailed advice to young man from the city (7)
- 24 How 15 ends up as a number in the trial (6)
- 26 A port prepared for a storm (5)

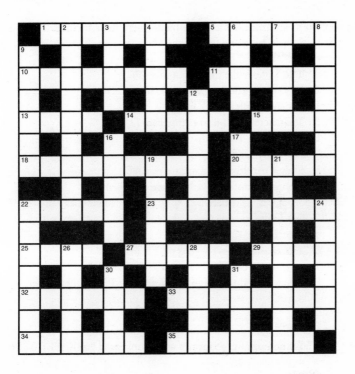

28 I care about Heather (5)
30 See 29
31 God's authority in part (4)

Eight solutions are from the same writer and are partially clued.

ACROSS

9 The writer's like this about love (9)

10 Returning setter's a drug as a friend (2,3)

11 Servant girl, a ludo player (5)

12 Thatcher's claim to the long lane (2,7)

13,6 Drops, say, frequently slip into post-revolutionary excess (5,2,6)

14 of 22,7 Host instinct of Virgin Mary displayed (7 of 7,8)

15 Lady Chatterley's opening is novel (7)

17 Picture bathe with Brahe being curtailed (7)

20 Total, say, or otherwise (7)

22 See 14ac

24 See 23

26 The elephant 'ain't saying nuffin' (5)

27 Two short – total other way (5)

28 Result of ignorance, maybe – so sew? Put the champagne back outside (9)

DOWN

1 Ecstasy uplifted Nureyev when embraced by friend: with this he won't feel a thing (8)

2 Cancel one of the rings (6)

3 Came down without, say, following 18 (8)

4 Fat villain with nut of nuts formed inside (5,5)

5 See the late-espoused the poet saw following 18 (4)

6 See 13

7 See 14ac

8 The last soldier in an illustration of a firework (6)

14 Quack with two plants (10)

16 Come to my house if you want any help from local men (4,2,2)

18 Show about lives (8)

19 Sussex town owns hose (8)

20 A spanner causing chaos (6)

21 Fish left in eminence, perhaps (6)

23,24 14ac before long holds horse: insist on directions (6,9)

25 Garment where we were marching? (4)

Clues which are in quotes are of a kind, and so are their solutions.

ACROSS

9 'Come, Proteus, 'tis your penance to season a dead brother's love' (9)
10 Love takes flight, as is due (5)
11 'I am that merry wanderer of the night: my master … is come in at your back door' (5)
12 'She is a woman, therefore may be wooed: O let me kiss this princess of pure white' (9)
13 Your noble Italian family has a name for the banquet in Titus Andronicus (9)
14 A lower Jurassic Balthazar was 6's (5)
16 'Whom I with this obedient steel … can lay to bed for ever, if the Jew do cut but deep enough' (7)
19 I have many enemies in Orsino's court – boys, apes, braggarts, Jacks, milksops! (7)
21 'My temple stands in Ephesus: when midnight comes, knock at my chamber window' (5)
23 'My brother's daughter's Queen of Tunis.' 'I never had a brother' (9)
26 Mother's bearing in Lily's place at a Spanish dance (9)
27 'This woman most wrongfully accused your substitute; then music with her silver sound … doth lend redress' (5)
28 Lot for lot, at random (5)
29 Surviving's about a hundred and one means of stimulation (9)

DOWN

1 Zero distance to Moscow river and on Norfolk coast (10)
2 Man, perhaps, with network (3,3)
3 One sister and one boy producing the same notes (2,6)
4,8 Time for little biters to accept bad deal (6,4)
5 Bird and bloke with one to one Wimbledon phenomenon (8)
6 'Unfold to me, your self, your half, why you are heavy: lay bare your bosom' (6)
7 Split gives 21 foresight (8)
8 See 4
15 Tin end for 25, but I'm making no promises (10)
17 Cate (who is spelt wrong) reluctant to be taken in hand at the sink (3,5)

18 Comparatively rude part of play little brother's upset about (8)
20 Returning drunkard observes more like himself (8)
22 'That is the chain, sir, which you had of me: this will last out a night in Russia' (6)
24 'O Cassio, Cassio, Cassio! Am I your bird? I mean to shift my bush' (6)
25 Mean home nurse (6)
26 'They have been at a great feast of languages, and stolen the scraps: and I ... Hail!' (4)

ACROSS

1,7 27's flower came from Grantchester (10,4)

9 Stairs of the 14 if 27's (6)

10,13 27's ending of letter from journalist no 1 (1,7,4)

11 Tennis player from 5 island at a little one (8)

12 Quite enough of page supplied by library at its closing? (6)

13 See 10

15 Tours leader remembered in Argentina where burrowing bird hasn't died (3,6)

17 Make up what occurs with TNT explosion (9)

20 See 5

21 Composer to put in boat (6)

23 I cry aloud and receive cold comfort (3,5)

25 Cat's coat may not be smooth (8)

26 This lot has a half of 27's work (3,3)

27 Flower with apple (4)

28 27's 17 on the beach (10)

DOWN

2 Avoid, first to last, a watercourse in India (5)

3 Considered what bass could be (7)

4 On a journey by Ford van? (2,7)

5,20ac 27's new tail, original head being lost (7,4)

6 Stay in bed giving place to piano (3,2)

7 Stagger, given shock treatment, and appoint current incumbent? (2-5)

8 Second little number put before the Queen as inducement (9)

14 Witch in French anteroom (9)

16 Genuine relation keeping the first cool (9)

18 Observes 'Anything but 23s' (7)

19 27's beast gets a place to study hackneyed stuff (7)

20 Cultivated areas are good for forests (7)

22 Stake-out to find poet (5)

24 27's work with other article given by phone (1,4)

Solve the clues and fit the solutions into the grid jigsaw-wise, wherever they will go.

A 'Ere's where some people resort, and a great one was Betsey to C (4)

B Sampson the lawyer of Q or his Sally acquires LSD (5)

C Sphere of police operations, loved Dora and made Agnes wait (11)

D Worthy of French allocation of food to be put on one's plate (9)

E Down with the duck? The reverse could be wider with change of direction (5)

F Ferrets, dear solver, are creatures that don't in the least want protection (4-7)

G Fact lover fell on Hard Times, for whom Spooner wrote 'diagram splendid' (9)

H Slab with which whelk is on offer – to sporting birds' legs they're appended (9)

I One with a night further South is accustomed to regions more polar (5)

J Burglar's accessory telling to Pickwick the tale of the stroller (5)

K Man of the law in Bleak House wrote King's English at end of his life (5)

L Plushy for Liberal head not exactly too fond of his wife (9)

M Muntle first gets new Italian name served by Nickleby (Kate) (9)

N Pleasant princess, so they say, is inclusive of Passover date (5)

O Paying no heed when commanding the view of the toilet attendant (11)

P Be economical, Tom – who was Pecksniff's too loyal dependant (5)

Q Joke about student and dwarf in The Old Curiosity Shop (5)

R Jew in Our Mutual Friend must have backing of cover on top (4)

S Teller of much in Bleak House has a season with chap next in line (9)

T Man of the law in that very same book, 'uge and 'eavy in spine (11)

U Ruin that comes to retriever deprived of beginning and end (4)

V Love is why creatures get stuffed, as you read in Our Mutual Friend (5)

W British without a success, here's a wash that's a total defeat (`5)

X Team that has training for gym – greet (say) E in it – fish that we eat (9)

Y Train destination in film: has the solver no love for his mother? (4)

Z Right from the Congo once keeping allegro, the point of another (9)

SOLUTIONS

Perimeter: IT IS, TOO/ HARD <A> KNOT(t)/ FOR M/E TO <U>N/TIE (*Twelfth Night* II.2.42).

1 AIR-BRICK
2 A/L P/AC/I/NO
3 AM/BASS/A/DOR
4 ASTR/ONOM/ER
5 CAP/A
6 CESAR/I/O
7 EL ADEM (hidden)
8 ER/IE
9 ILSE (anag)
10 IRIS/H SE/A
11 I/SOP/T/ERA
12 LIT/HOG/RAP/H
13 MIS(s)/READ
14 N<AIR>OB/I

15 NATURE
16 NUNN (none)
17 OLIVIA (anag)
18 'OP<HIT>E
19 OR/SIN/O
20 OTT/AWA
21 RACK/RENT
22 REEF
23 STRAITS
24 T/EMPERER
25 TOPOL/OGIST
26 TRUE TO LIFE (anag)
27 TSAR (hidden)
28 UNDERSPENT (anag)

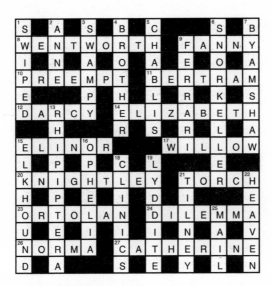

Theme: Brides in Jane Austen's novels.

ACROSS

8 WEN<TWO/RT>/H
9 FAN/NY
10 PRE-EMPT (anag)
11 BERTRAM (Wooster)
12 DA<RC>Y
14 E/LIZA(Maugham)/ (Lam)BETH
15 ELIN<O>/R (rev)
17 WILL/OW(e) (*Twelfth Night* I.5.288)
20 K<NIGH/TL(thallium, atomic t)>EY
21 TOR/CH
23 OR/TO<LA>N
24 (croco)DILE/M/MA
26 NORMA
27 CA<THE/R>INE

DOWN

1 SWIPED
2 (t)ANNE(r)
3 SWA<MP>Y
4 B/ROT/HER
5 CHA/BLIS
6 SNOR(e)/KELLER
7 (Glen) BY/AM/ SHAW
9 (sa)F<ERR>ARI
13 R/HIPIP/T/ERA
15 ELKHOUND (anag)
16 OPH(of)/ELIA
18 C/L/IN/ICS
19 LY(u)DDITE
21 TIL/NEY (all rev)
22 H<E>AVEN (Drake's drum)
25 MAIL

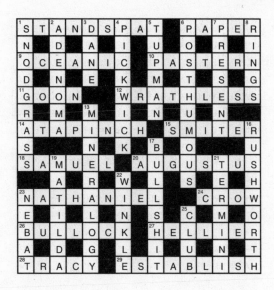

Title: Mr Jingle's comment on first seeing the badge (PC) of the …
Posthumous Papers of the Pickwick Club.

ACROSS

1 ST/AND/S PAT
6 PAPER
9 OCEAN/I/C (ceano/thus)
10 PA/STERN
11 GO/ON
12 WRATHLESS (anag)
14 A/T A/ PINCH
15 SMITER (anag)
18 SA<M>U<E>L
20 AUGUSTUS (Struwwelpeter)
23 NA/THAN<I>E/L
24 CROW
26 B<UL>LOCK
27 HEL(L)IER
28 TRA<C>Y
29 E<STAB>LISH(a)

DOWN

1 SNOD(rev)/GRASS
2 ADEN/OMA(n)
3 DANE (hidden)
4 PICK/WICK (ed)
5 TUP/MAN
6 POSTHUM<O>US
7 PRESENT
8 RINGS
13 MINERALOGY (anag)
16 RUSH/WORTH
17 BULLS/HIT
19 MATILDA
21 TERMINI (anag)
22 WINKLE
23 NEBAT (Jeroboam – I Kings)
25 CLUB

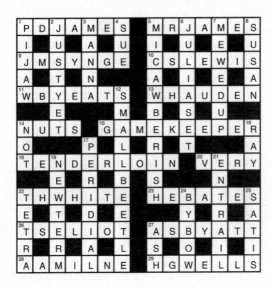

(7) solutions are really (1,1,5); they are writers of five letters usually referred to by their two initials.

ACROSS

1   P D JAMES (claSPED MAJor)
5   M R JAMES (foR EMMA'S Jaunt)
9   J M SYNGE (synoNYMS E G Jane's)
10 C S LEWIS (exCESS WILl)
11 W B YEATS (bABY WESTon)
13 W H AUDEN (MorlAND WE HUmbly)
14 NUTS
15 GAME/KEEPER
18 TEN/DER-/LO/IN
20,12 VERY SMALL BEETLE (Winnie the Pooh: Stalky)
22 T H WHITE (WITH THE)
23 H E BATES (wAS THE BEnnets')
26 T S ELIOT (a lITTLE SOmething)
27 A S BYATT (STAY AT Bath)
28 A A MILNE (coloNEL AMIAble)
29 H G WELLS (admiraL'S LEG WHich)

DOWN

1   P<(d)IJ(on)>AW
2   See 14
3   MANNA (manor)
4   SUE
5   MICAWBERISH (anag)
6   JULIA/ SET
7   MEWED/UP
8   S<USA>N
12 See 20
14,2 NOT JUST YET
16 RAY
17 PERI/DIAL
19 NEW TERM
21 ENT/RAIL
22 TETRA (hidden)
24 BY-B(l)OW
25 SAT/IS
27 ASH

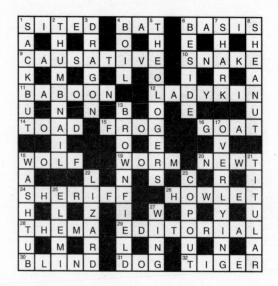

Theme: The witches' cauldron (*Macbeth* IV.1).

ACROSS

1 SITED (sighted)
4 BAT
6 BeAnS/IS
9 CA<USA/TI>VE
10 SNAKE
11 B<AB>OON
12 LA<DYK(e)>IN
14 T<O>AD
15 FROG
16 GOAT
18 WOLF
20 NEWT
24 SHE/RIFF
26 HOW/LET
28 (ana)THEMA
29 EDITORIAL (anag)
30,19 BLINDWORM
31 DOG
32 TIGER

DOWN

1 SACK/BUT(t)
2 THUMBNAIL
3 DRAG/ON
4 BOIL
5 THEOLOGERS (anag)
6 BE<SID>E
7 SH/ARK
8 SHEA NUT (anag)
13 BROWN/FIELD
17 OVER/LYING
18 WASHTUB (anag)
21 TIT/U/LAR(k)
22 LIZARD
23 CO/P-OUT
25 ELE/MI
27 WIN/G

Perimeter: NIGHTMARE ABBEY and CROTCHET CASTLE (Thomas Love Peacock).

1 (ylr)AEN/EID (all rev)
2 ARMA/LITE
3 AWHILE (anag)
4 C-IN-C/TURE(en)
5 COD/A
6 CUSP(idor)
7 ENOSIS (anag)
8 FLOPPY DISC (anag)
9 F<LU J>AB
10 FL<Y H>AUNT (Ode to N'gale)
11 GUI/DANCE
12 See 13
13,12 HEADLONG/ HALL
14 HE<LP>ED

15 I/CON
16 MEL/IN/COURT
17 N<A>OUS/A
18 NIGHTS (anag)
19 NINE(nein)-/INCH
20 NINNY'S TOMB (MND – Flu/te)
21 ONE FINE DAY
22 PHARISEE (hidden)
23 RE<E>FER
24 REI(g)NED
25 T<HR>ONE
26 TON(t)ALITY
27 TREATY
28 USEDN'T (anag)

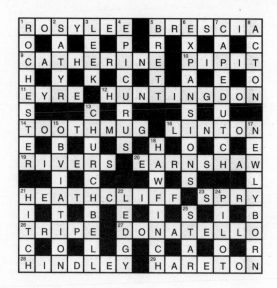

Theme: Brontë novels.

ACROSS

1 ROSY(ie) LEE (Laurie)
5 BRESCIA (anag)
9 CATHERINE
10 PIP/IT
11 EYR(i)E
12 HUNTING/DON
14 TOOTH/ MUG
16 LIN/TON (rev)
19 RIVERS
20 EARNS/HAW
21 HEATH/CLIFF
23 SPRY
26 TRIP/E
27 DON/A(rev)/TELL/O
28 HIND/LEY
29 HARE/TON

DOWN

1 ROCHESTER
2 SATYR (anag)
3 LEEK (leak)
4 EPIC/UR/US
5 BRETT(on) (*Villette*)
6 EXPANSIONS (axe pensions)
7 CA<PE D/U>TCH
8 ACT/ON
13 CHURCH/ BELL
15 OBVIATION (anag)
17 NEWLY <BOR(rev)>N
18 HAWFINCH (anag)
21 HITCH
22 L/EDGY
24 PILOT
25 STAR (rats)

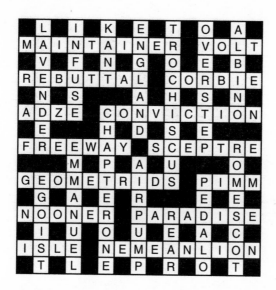

Perimeter: LIKE TO A TENEMENT OR PELTING FARM (*Richard II* II.1.60).

1 ADZE (ads)
2 AI/R-<P>UMP
3 A/LB/IN/O
4 C<HAPTER ON>E
5 CONVICTION
6 CORBIE (Corby)
7 EG/'OIST
8 EMMA/NU/EL
9 ENGLAND
10 FR<EEW(rev)>AY
11 GEOMETRIDS (anag)
12 IN/FUSE
13 ISLE (hidden)
14 K/ANT

15 LAV<END>ER
16 MAIN/TAINER(anag)
17 NE<MEAN/ LI>ON
18 NOONE/R
19 OVER/STEP
20 PARAD<IS>E
21 PEDALO (anag)
22 PI/MM
23 REAR
24 RE<BUTT>AL
25 ROME-SCOT (anag)
26 SCEPT(ical)/RE
27 TROCHISCUS (anag)
28 (re)VOLT

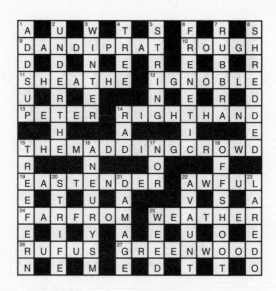

ACROSS

9   DANDI/PRAT
10,25   ROUGH WEATHER (anag)
11   SHE/AT/HE
12,20   IG(rev)/NO/BLE ST/RIFE
13   PETER
14   RIGHT-HAND
15   See 24
19   EAS<TEND>ER
22   (l)AWFUL
24,15   FAR FROM THE M/ADDING/
      CROWD (Gray and Hardy)
25   See 10
26   RUF(roof)/US
27   See 2

DOWN

1   A/DD/S UP
2,27,4   UNDER THE GREENWOOD
      TREE (anag) (Shakespeare and
      Hardy)
3   WINTER (hidden)
4   See 2
5   ST/RING
6   FREN<ETI>C(h)
7   RUB/BRA
8   SHREDDED
14,17   RAD/NO/R
15   T/REE FER/N
16   ANEURYSM (anag)
17   See 14
18   OFF/SHOOT
20   See 12
21   DAM/AGE
22   A/VAUNT
23   L/ARE/DO
25   WEED

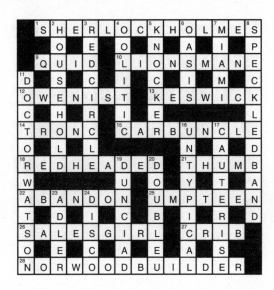

ACROSS

1 SHER/LOCK <HOLM>E'S
9 QUID
10 LION'S MANE
12 OWENIST (anag)
13 KES/WICK
14 TRONC (hidden)
15 CARBUNCLE
18 RED-HEADED
21 THUMB
22 A/BAND/ON
25 U/MP/TEEN
26 SALES GIRL (anag)
27 CRIB
28 NORWOOD BUILDER (anag)

DOWN

2 HOUSE/HOLD
3 RED/ CIRCLE
4 OO/LIT/I/C
5 KNOCKER
6 O/AS/IS
7 MIA/MI
8 SPEC/K/LED/ BAND
11 DO<CT>OR/ W(h)AT'S/ON
16 UNTYPICAL (anag)
17 CAU(gh)T/(h)ER/ISE(eyes)
19 DUN/CI<A>D
20 D'OU/BLE-U (Fr)
23 (Irene) ADLER (*Scandal in Bohemia*)
24 DI'S/CO

Perimeter: NATIVE HERE AND TO THE MANNER BORN (*Hamlet* I.4.14).

1 AD/VICE
2 BRA/VERY
3 CONVENTION
4 CU'S/TOM
5 ES<TEEM>ED
6 ETHICS (anag)
7 EYE/TEETH
8 HO<NO>UR
9 I/(ga)SOLINE
10 MORE
11 NODDER
12 NOVEMBER (anag)
13 NUMINOUS (anag)
14 O<BSERVA(anag)>NCE

15 O/UTG/UN (III.5.3)
16 O/VERB/OLD (*Macbeth* III.5.3)
17 PERDITA (anag)
18 RESI/DUAL(duel)
19 R/OAR
20 SLIP-S/HOE
21 TAL(l)/BOT(but)
22 T<OODLE>-OO
23 TREMOR (hidden)
24 TRIUM(ph)/V/IR
25 (pi)TY/BALT
26 UNLOOSE (anag)
27 VIRGI(n)/LIA(rev)
28 VI/R/TUE

Perimeter: OUR LITTLE SYSTEMS HAVE THEIR DAY (anag)
(Tennyson, *In Memoriam*, prologue).

1 (sub)ALTERN
2 DITT<AN>Y
3 DYER (dier)
4 E/FF<US>ION
5 HAL/LAM
6 H<A/RE-F>OOT
7 HOOD-<MOULD>S
8 IN MEM/OR/I/AM
9 IRIDOSMIUM (anag)
10 LAHS (anag)
11 LETTISH (lettuce)
12 LITTLE/NESS
13 OAK/LEY
14 OCEAN LEVEL (anag)

15 PE<NU>LT
16 PIA/NO/(p)LA(y)
17 PUSH
18 RHETORS (anag)
19 RO(w)AN
20 SLAE (anag)
21 TEA/L
22 TENNYS/ON
23 TREE LINE
24 UN/DE
25 UND<ERR>ATED
26 VISIONLE(anag)/SS
27 V<OR/OS/HILO>V
28 YAW/N

Perimeter: WHAT WAS HE DOING, THE GREAT GOD PAN? (down in the reeds by the river) (E B Browning, *A Musical Instrument*).

1 AB/ET
2 'A BIT/CH
3 AIR/ STRIKES
4 A/MULE/T
5 BROKEN REED
6 BY THE RIVER (anag)
7 CO/C<KS>URE
8 DEPENDABLE (anag)
9 DE<SPIT>E
10 DOWNING
11 GALA/TIAN(anag)
12 HE'LL
13 LOTH(ario)
14 NIGH/T <D>OG (*Merry Wives* end)

15 NO/VE<MB>ER
16 OR/ANGE-R/OOT
17 POND (hidden)
18 RE/ALIA
19 SC/ARCE
20 SEMI(tic)
21 SPOKE TO (Spoleto)
22 T<ILL>IE
23 T<OM/MY>ROT
24 TRAC/TOR (all rev)
25 WAGE
26 WATCHED POT (anag)
27 WELWYN (well in)
28 WO<RM/HOL>E

136

A	C	R	O	S	S		M	A	D	R	I	G	A	L
I		O		I		I		U		E		U		A
R	H	Y	M	E		N	A	R	R	A	T	I	O	N
B		A		V		F		I		D		T		D
A	L	L	S	E	E	I	N	G		Y	E	A	T	S
G		W		L		D		A				R		E
	P	E	R	I	G	E	E		L	E	S	S	E	N
T			K		L		E		X					D
U	N	D	I	E	S		A	P	P	O	I	N	T	
C		R			A		I		N		O			S
K	A	Y	L	E		C	A	T	H	E	D	R	A	L
S		W		R		T		O		R		O		E
H	E	A	D	G	R	O	O	M		A	N	D	R	E
O		L		O		N		E		T		O		V
P	A	L	M	T	R	E	E		G	E	M	M	A	E

GLAMIS hath MURDERED SLEEP and therefore CAWDOR shall SLEEP NO MORE, Macbeth shall SLEEP NO MORE.

1 A/CROSS
2 AC/T ONE
3 A/(le)IRBAG(rev)
4 ALL-SEEING
5 ANDRE (hidden)
6 AP<POIN(s)>T
7 AURIGA (Capella)
8 CAT/HE<DR>AL
9 DRY WALL
10 EPITOME (anag)
11 ER/GOT
12 EX/ONE/RATE
13 GEMMAE (jimmy)
14 GUITARS (anag)
15 HEAD <G>ROOM
16 INFIDEL (anag)
17 KAYLE (anag)
18 LAND'S END
19 LESSEN (lesson)
20 MAD/RIGA/L
21 N/ARRA<TIO>N
22 NO<ROD>OM
23 PALM TREE
24 PERI/GEE
25 REA<D>Y (anag)
26 RHYME
27 RO<YAL(rev)>WE
28 SI<EVE-LI(na)>KE(s)
29 SLEEVE
30 TUCK S/HOP(e)
31 UN/DIES
32 Y/EATS

Perimeter: ALL THE (anag)/ DROWSY SYRUPS OF THE WORLD (anag) (*Othello* III.3.332).

1 BLEW(blue)/A/WAY
2 CI<TAD>EL
3 ETIENNE (anag)
4 EYED (I'd)
5 FLEW (flu)
6 FREE CREDIT (freak read it)
7 FR<O[W]Z>Y
8 HOOD
9 HOUSE MOUSE
10 MAN/DRAGO(n)/RA
11 O DE/ATH (where is thy s.)
12 ON THE GRASS (anag)
13 OPI(e)/ATE
14 ORS/IN/O

15 OT<HELL>O
16 PYOT (hidden)
17 RA/IN-DO<CT>OR
18 RE<SELECTE>D
19 RESOURCE
20 SAND/WELL
21 S<K>OL
22 SWEET SLEEP (sweep sleet)
23 T/HE <AN>GEL
24 THRE<E/ HE>ADS (triceps)
25 TIME (in prison)
26 (t)UBEROUS
27 WEE/P
28 YARE

138

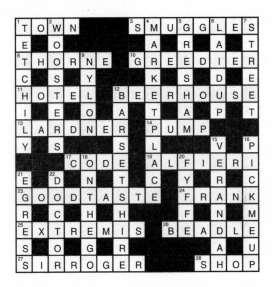

Title: *Doctor Thorne* is the third of Trollope's five 'chronicles of Barset'.

ACROSS

1 TOW/N
3 S/MUGGLES
8 See 22
10 GREE<DIE>R
11 HOT/EL
12 BEE/R-<H>OUSE
13 L(e)AR<D>NER
14 PUMP
17 COD/E
19 AL<F>I(ghi)ERI
23 GOOD TASTE (anag)
24,5 F<RANK/ G>RESH/AM
25 EXTREMIS(t)
26 BE<ADL>E
27 SIR ROGER (de Coverley)
28 SH/OP

DOWN

1 TET/CHIL(l)Y
2 WOOSTERS (anag)
4 MARKETPLACE (anag)
5 See 24
6 L<AID> UP(in)
7 S<TREE>T
9 NY/LON(don)
12 BAR/SETS/HIRE
15 VE<RAND>AH
16 PICK-ME-UP
18 (m)ON TH/E GO
20 FYFFE (Fife)
21 (n)EGRESS
22,8 DOC<TOR T/HORN>E

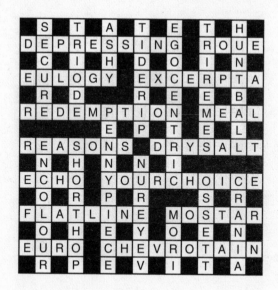

Perimeter: STATE THE ALTERNATIVE PREFERRED (with REASONS for YOUR CHOICE).

1 A/SHY
2 CHEVRO<TA/I>N
3 C<RAN>IA
4 D<EP>RESSING
5 DRY-SALT (anag)
6 ECHO (hidden)
7 E<GO/CENT>RIC
8 ENCOLOUR (anag)
9 EULOGY (anag)
10 EURO (hidden)
11 EXCE<R>PT/A
12 F<LATL>INE
13 HUNT BALL (golf)
14 MEAL

15 MORI
16 MO/STAR
17 NUR/EYE/V (all rev)
18 OSSET/T, OS/SETT
19 PENNY-/PIECE (peace)
20 REASONS
21 REDEMPTION (anag)
22 RO(g)UE
23 SE/CURE
24 SHORT/ HOP
25 T<IDE> RIP
26 TRIODE (anag)
27 TRIREMES (try reams)
28 YOU/R <(e)CHO>ICE

Perimeter: I AM CONSTANT/ AS/ THE NORTHERN STAR (*Julius Caesar* II.1.60).

1 AL(l)/COCK
2 ALPH/ABET
3 See 16
4 BALA(nce)
5 B/A/UBLE
6 BONESET
7 BORN(e)
8 B<RUT>US
9 CAD/WALADER (anag)
10 CAS<SI>US
11 COURT-BARON (anag)
12 E<A/SINE>SS
13 ELAH (rev)
14 E<XP>LICIT
15 I WILL REPAY (Romans 12.19) (title of book)

16,3 MAR<K ANTON>Y
17 NAVI(rev)/GATE
18 NYM/P/HAL/IDS
19 OPERATIONS
20 OVER/L<A>UNCH
21 PICAS/SO
22 RELICT (anag)
23 RE/SIN/AT/A
24 R<WAND>A
25 S/AR<DIN>IA
26 SE/MI
27 SP/READS
28 TROY

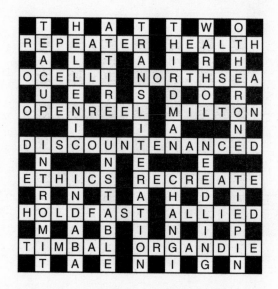

Perimeter: THAT TWO-HANDED (anag) ENGINE AT THE DOOR stands ready to strike once and strike no more (*Lycidas* l.130).

1 AL/LIED
2 ATTIRE (a tyre)
3 CHANG(e)/I
4 DISCOUNT/E/NANCED(anag)
5 ETHICS (anag)
6 HEA<L>TH
7 HELL/ENIC
8 HOLD FAST
9 IN/DAB/A
10 IN/TROM/IT
11 MIL/TON
12 NEED/LING
13 NORTH SEA (anag)

14 O/CELLI(st)
15 OPEN-REEL (anag)
16 ORGAN/DIE
17 OT<HER ON>E
18 RE/CRE<A>TE
19 REP/EATER
20 TEAC(teak)/UP
21 THIRD MAN
22 TIEPIN (typin')
23 TIM/BAL
24 TRANSLITERATION (anag)
25 (d)UNSTABLE
26 WAR/HOL

Title from Wordsworth, 'Lines Written in Early Spring'.

ACROSS

1 TAMORA (*Titus Andronicus* I.1.450)

4 VIRGILIA (*Coriolanus* I.3.42)

10 PETRUCHIO (*The Taming of the Shrew* II.1/192) (do. 195)

11 BAGOT (*Richard II* IV.1.6)

12 CELIA (*As You Like It* I.2.113)

13 BRABANTIO (*Othello* I.2.62)

14 SAMPSON (*Romeo and Juliet* I.1.56)

16 HAMLET (*Hamlet* III.4.134)

19 ARTHUR (*King John* IV.1.39)

21 GONERIL (*King Lear* III.7.5)

23 ENOBARBUS (*Anthony and Cleopatra* II.2.206)

25 CURIO (*Twelfth Night* I.1.16)

27 EGEUS (*A Midsummer Night's Dream* I.1.22)

28 CLEOPATRA (*Anthony and Cleopatra* IV.13.67)

29 SALARINO (*The Merchant of Venice* I.1.47)

30 ALONSO (*The Tempest* II.1.118)

DOWN

1 TYPECAST (anag)

2 METAL (hidden) (*Hamlet* III.2.117)

3 R/OU<MANS>CH

5 I/SO/BATH

6 GAB/BA (Sydney ground)

7 LIGHT-YEAR (anag)

8 ACT/I/ON

9 THE/BAN

15 M<ARMOR>EAL

17 MUNIC(h)/I/PAL

18 ELDORADO (anag) (Chapman's Homer)

20 RUB/ICON

21 G<ASK>ET

22 RECESS

24 ANS(w)ER

26 RAT (i)ON

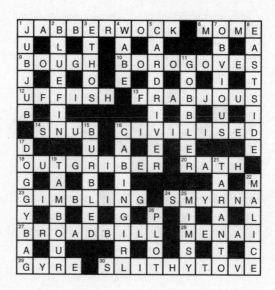

See *Through the Looking Glass*, chapters 1 and 6.

ACROSS

- *1 JABBER/WOCK(wok)
- *6,20 MOME RATH (anag)
- 9 BOUGH (bow) (Cheshire c)
- *10 BOR<O/GOV>ES
- *12 UFFI/SH(z/i)
- *13 FRA<BJO(anag)>US
- 14 SNUB (buns)
- 16 C<I/V/I/L>ISED
- *18 OUTG<RIB>ER(anag)
- 20 See 6
- *23 GIMBLING
- 24 SMYRNA (anag)
- 27 BRO<AD/>BILL
- 28 MEN/AI
- *29 GYRE
- *30 SLI<THY> TOVE

DOWN

- *1 JU<B>JUB(es)
- 2 BL<UEF(rev)>IN(d)
- 3 E/THO(ma)S
- *4 W/ABE
- 5 CAR D/RIVER
- 7 OB/V/IOUS
- 8 EAS<T SID(rev)>E
- 11 GOBBLER
- *15 (y)BUR(rev)/BLED
- 16 C<A/BIN G(e)>IRL
- 17 DO/GG/Y-BA/G
- 19 TAMBO/UR
- 21 TA/RAN/TO
- 22 M/ALICE
- *25 M<I/MS>Y
- 26 PLOT

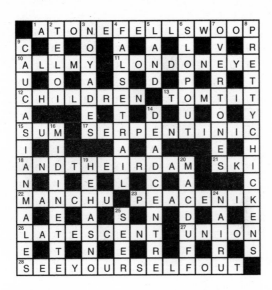

See *Macbeth* IV.3.216–8.

ACROSS

1　AT ONE/ FELL S/WOO/P
10,8,18　ALL MY PRETTY CHICKENS
　　　AND THEIR DAM (anag)
11　LO/N<DON E>YE
12　See 19
13　TO/MT/IT
15　SUM (some)
17　SER<PENT>IN/IC
18　See 10
21　SKI
22　MAN/CHU (chew)
23　PEA<(i)CENI>K
26　LATE/SCENT
27　UNION
28　SEE YOURSELF/ OUT

DOWN

2　TELOI(v) (rev)
3　NO<YAD(rev)>ES
4　FALSE TRAIL (anag)
5,25　LAND/SEER
6　SLO<P O/U>T
7　OVERT/ONES
8　See 10
9　CAUC(us)/AS/I/AN M/ALES
14　DEAD CENTRE
16　MI/DINETTE
19,12　HE HAS NO CHILDREN
20　M<A/CD>UFF
24　NAIRU (hidden)
25　See 5

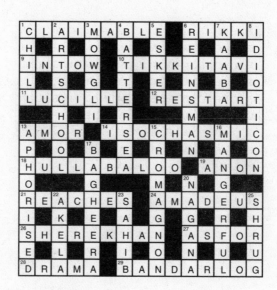

Theme: JUN<GLE BO/O>K.

ACROSS

1 C<LAIM>ABLE
6,10 RIKK/I/-TIK/KI-T/AVI
9 IN TO/W
10 See 6
11 LUC<ILL>E
12 REST/ART
13 A/MOR
14 I/S<O/CHASM>IC
18 HULL/A/BALOO
19 ANON
21 RE-ACHES
24 A/MADE/US
26 SH/ERE KHAN (anag)
27 AS FOR (anag)
28 DRAM/A
29 B<AND/AR>LOG

DOWN

1 CHIL/L
2 ART SCHOOL (anag)
3 MOW/GLI(s)
4 BATTER/SEA
5 ESK/E/R
6 REINSMAN (anag)
7 KAA/BA
9 IDIOT/ICON
13 AP<H[OR]IS>ED
15 C/ROMAGN(a)/ON
16 MANGERFUL (anag)
17 BAG/HE/ERA
20 NAG/A(i)NA
22 AKELA (hidden)
23 SA/HIB
25 SH/RUG

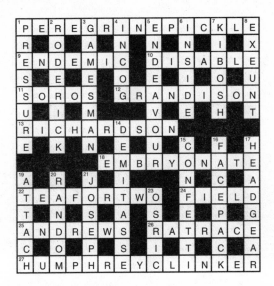

Theme: (Tobias) S<MOLL>ETT.

ACROSS

1   PEREGRINE/ PICKLE
9   EN<DEMI>C
10 DI/SABLE
11 SOROS (sorrows)
12 GRAND<I>SON
13 RICH/ARDSON(anag)
18 E-M<BRYON(y)>ATE
22 TEA FOR TWO (anag)
24 FIELD(ing)
25 See 21
26 RA/T RACE
27 HUMPHREY(sic)/ CLINKER

DOWN

1   PRESSURE
2,20 RODE/RICK(shaw)/ RAN/DO/M
3   GAM<ES>MA/N
4   IN/COG
5   ENDEAV<O>UR (anag)
6   IN/SIDE
7   K/I/BOSH (dish vb.)
8   EXE/UNT
14   DEMI<TAS>SE
15   CONFETTI (anag)
16   FACE/ PACK
17   HE<ADGE>AR
19   ATT<AC>H(anag)
20   See 2
21,25 JOSEPH ANDREWS (anag)
23   OS/RIC (hidden) (*Hamlet* V.2.84)

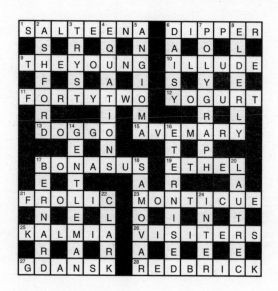

'Peaple' is Daisy Ashford's spelling.

ACROSS

1 SALTEENA (anag)
6 DIPPER
9,26 THE YOUNG VISITERS (anag)
10 I<LLUD(rev)>E
11 FORTY-TWO (fortitude)
12 Y<OG>URT
13 DOG/GO
15 AV<E M(rev)(i)>ARY
17 BON<A/S>US
19,23 ET<HEL M>ON/T/I/CUE
21 FRO(h)LIC(h)
23 See 19
25 KALMIA (anag)
26 See 9
27 G(o)D/A<N>SK
28 RED/BRICK

DOWN

2 See 6
3 TRY/ST
4 EQUATIONS (anag)
5 AN<GI/OM>A
6,2 DAISY/ ASH/FORD
7 P<O(i)>LYGRAPH (anag)
8 EL/DER/L/Y
14 GE<N/TLEM(rev)>AN
16 E<TERN/IS>ED(rev)
17,22 BE<RN>ARD/ C/LARK
18 SAM/OVA/R
20 LAU/TREC (low trek)
22 See 17
24 (w)INTER

HARK HARK THE WATCH-DOGS BARK: BOW WOW (*The Tempest* I.2.381).

1 A/B/RAM
2 ATHLETE'S FOOT
3 BLOG(G)S
4 BL/OTTO
5 CAIN (cane)
6 COTTESLOE (anag)
7 CR<E/SCENT/ M>OON
8 D<A/CO>IT
9 EG/G<AR M>OTH
10 EV<OK>E
11 FINE GAEL (anag)
12 FRENCH
13 GLUT/A/MATE
14 GROW/L
15 HIGHER (hire – purchase)

16 KERMES (anag)
17 LAR<CE/N>OUS(se)
18 LONGEST (art longing)
19 OGRE (hidden)
20 (h)ORNER/Y
21 RE-IGN(ite)(ms)
22 SO/N<OR>OUS
23 ST/ITCH
24 SUN/DEW
25 T/CHICK
26 THIRTY (tennis)
27 T<ONSO>RIAL
28 TWEE/TER
29 UNCL<OTH>ES
30 U<NWO(rev)>RN

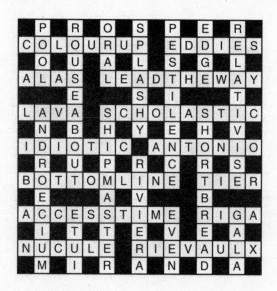

Perimeter: PROSPER(o), MIRANDA, CALIBAN, SYCORAX (*The Tempest*).

1 AC<CESS TI>ME
2 A/LAS(s)
3 AND/ROE/CIUM(s)(anag)
4 ANT/ON/IO
5 BOTTOM LINE (*A Midsummer Night's Dream* III.1.87)
6 CO<LO/UR> UP
7 ED/DIES
8 EDGE (hidden)
9 ET/U/I
10 EVEN
11 GALA(had)
12 I/DIOTIC
13 LA(r)VA
14 LEAD THE WAY (anag)

15 NU/CULE (new cool)
16 (past)ORAL
17 PE<STILE>NCE
18 POOL
19 RE<LATIV(rev)>ISE(anag)
20 RI<EVAUL>X
21 RIG/A
22 RIV(rev)/I/ERA
23 ROU/SEA/BOUT
24 SCHOLASTIC (anag)
25 SHIPMASTER (anag)
26 SHORT/BREAD
27 S/PLA<SH>Y
28 TIER

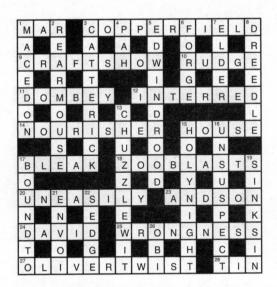

Title: Reference to *A CHRISTMAS CAROL*.

Theme: Dickens novels.

ACROSS

1,28,13 M<ART/IN/ CH>UZZLE/WIT
3 See 24
9 C<RAFT S>HOW
10 (beg) RUDGE
11,23 DO<M[BEY] AN>D SON (D&F, *Pickwick Papers*)
12 INTER/RED
14 NOURISHER (anag) (*Macbeth* II.2.41)
15 See 17
17,15 BL<E[A/K] H>OUSE
18 ZOO/BLASTS
20 UNEASILY (anag)
23 See 11
24,3 DAVID/ COPPER/FIELD
25 WRONGNESS (anag)
27 O<LIVER> T/WIST
28 See 1

DOWN

1 MACE/DON
2 REARM/OUSE
3 C<ATTE>RICK
4 PAH
5 ED/WIN D/ROOD
6 FORGE
7 ELDER
8 D<REED>LE (all rev)
13 See 1ac
15 H<OLY N>IGHT
16 UNSUSPECT (anag)
17 BOUND TO
19 SINK/S IN
21 ENVOI (hidden)
22 S/EDGE
26 OBI(t)

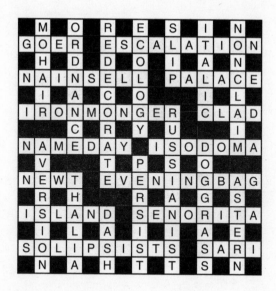

Perimeter: MORE S/INN/ED AG/A/INST/ TH<AN S>INNING (*King Lear* III.2.59).

1 AS/TERN	15 NA/IN/SELL
2 A/VERSION	16 NAME DAY
3 C/LAD	17 NEWT(on)
4 DASH	18 N/ON-CL(e)/AIM
5 DOG-G(e)R/ASS	19 ORD(i)NANCE
6 E<COLO>G/Y	20 P<A>LACE
7 E<SCA>LATION	21 PERSIST (anag)
8 EVENING BAG (anag)	22 REDE/C<O>RATE
9 G/O'ER	23 RUSSIANIST (anag)
10 IRONMONGER (anag)	24 SARI (Iras)
11 ISLAND	25 SE<NOR/IT>A
12 I/SODOMA	26 SLIP
13 ITALIC (hidden)	27 S<O>LIP/SI<S>TS
14 MO/HAIR	28 T<HAL>IA (rev)

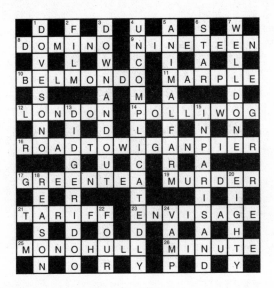

Theme: George Orwell novels.

ACROSS

8	DOMINO
9,20,22	NINETEEN-EIGHTY-FOUR
10	BEL/MONDO
11	MARPLE
12	See 3
14	POLL/I/W/OG
16	RO<AD/ TO/ WIG/AN> PIER
17	GR<EEN> TEA (anag)
19	MURDER (will out)
21	TA/RIFF
23	ENVISAGE (anag)
25	MO/NO/HULL (catamaran)
26	MINUTE

DOWN

1	DOVE S/O/NO
2,6	FILM STAR (anag)
3,15,12	DOWN AND OUT IN PARIS/ AND LONDON (anag)
4	UNCOMPLICATEDLY (anag)
5	A/NIM/AL <F>ARM
6	See 2
7	WEL<L> DON/E
13	DID/GERI/DO/O
15	See 3
18	RE/A/SON
20,22	See 9
24	V/AMP

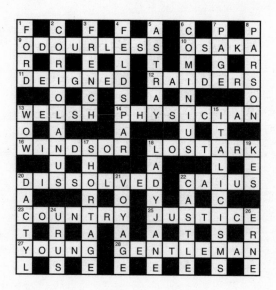

Theme: *Merry Wives of Windsor* – dramatis personae.

ACROSS

9 ODOURLESS (anag)
10 OS/AKA
11 DEIGNED (Dane'd)
12 R<A>IDERS
13,8 WELS(rev)/H P/ARSON
16,22 WINDS/OR CA'S/TLE
18 LO/ST ARK
20 DIS/SOLVED
22 CAIUS (keys)
23,25 COUNTRY/ JUST/ICE
27,28 YOUNG GENTLEMAN (Fenton)

DOWN

1 FORD
2 COR<IOLAN(the)>US
3,14 FRENCH PHYSICIAN (anag)
4 FELDSPAR (anag)
5 AS/TRAY
6 CO/MINI/US
7 P(ass)AGE
13 W<O>W
15 ITALICISMS
17 SHORT/AGE
18 LAD/Y <JAN>E
19 KES (hidden)
20 DACTYL
21 VOYAGE (anag)
24 UR(s)US
26 ERNE

Ecclesiastes ch3 v2–8: a TIME ... BORN, DIE; KILL, HEAL; CAST AWAY STONES, gather STONES TOGETHER; GET, LOSE; KEEP, CAST AWAY; REND, SEW; KEEP SILENCE, SPEAK; LOVE, HATE; WAR, PEACE.

ACROSS

1 BOR(o)N
4 LIGHT
12 RIDE
16 EM/BRACE (refrain from ...)
18 AM/BUSH
20 LATRIA (hidden)
22 WIT/HERS
24 WEE/P (laugh)
26 TRIP
30 SPEAKERS
32 A/BOUND
33 TIME
34 PEW/IT
35 NO/EL

DOWN

2 OUTCOME
3 NO<N-M>(v)EMBER
4 LOSER (hidden rev)
6 TOGA (anag)
7 HATER (anag)
8 AVER/NUS
15,17 CASTAWAY
19 BREAKDOWN (build up)
21 A/DELPHI
27 PLANT (pluck up ...)
31 S/E/W

Theme: Coleridge, *Kubla Khan*.

ACROSS

1 IN BED
4 CAP/IT/ELLA
9 CHAR/MEUSE
10 R/ALPH
11 NAIL
12 ABYSS/IN/IAN
14 EG/G NOG(rev)
15 ARRAN/GER
17 FLASHING
19 See 27
23 THICK/ PANTS
24 OVEN (hidden)
26 LUIGI (anag)
27,19 ANCESTRAL(anag)/ V<O>ICES
28 BEN/BE<CU(l)>LA
29 U/NSEW(anag)

DOWN

1,2 INCENSE/-BEARING
3 See 5
4 C/HUBBY
5,3 P<LEAS/U/RE-D>OME
6 TERMINATOR (anag)
7 LULLI/NG
8 (n)ATHAN/OR
13 TO THE KNIFE
16 IN <XANA(rev)>DU(s)
17 FAT S/LOB
18 (p) AVILION
20 C/AVERN(u)S
21 SUNG/LOW
22 A/T/O/C/I/A
25 ESAU (hidden)

Perimeter: (The cat would) EAT FISH BUT WOULD NOT WET HER FEET (anag) (see *Macbeth* I.7.44).

1 A/D<HER>ENT
2 A<R>ID
3 BAR<CAROL>LE(y)
4 BOTTOM ('rude m'., *A Midsummer Night's Dream*)
5 B/R/A/E
6 D/HOW
7 E<LEG/I>AST
8 ENIGMA
9 FACT/ICE
10 HOLLA(nd)-HOA(r)
11 IM/P/I
12 IN <BRIE>F
13 IN SHORT
14 See 24

15 LABRADOR
16 LORN (hidden)
17 MAN MAD(e)
18 MIN<D READ>ER
19 O/MAR
20 ON COMMAND/O
21 OPIE (hidden)
22 O/W<L>ISH
23 STE<AM/ POW>ER
24,14 THE PO/OR CA/T IN T/HE AD/ AGE
25 THREATENER (three tenor)
26 ULNA (hidden)
27 UNBLEACHED (anag)
28 WAR/WICK (Bear & ragged staff)

Theme: Contemporaries of Abraham Cowley, 'in his day considered the greatest of English poets' (*Chambers Biographical Dictionary*).

ACROSS

1 LESBIA/N
5 MAD<E> MAD
9 VA<CAT>ES
10 FIN/ALLY
11 ELI (hidden)
12 LILTING (little thing)
13 (p)OPE/ROSE
19,14 S<EVEN/TEE[N]TH> CENT/URY
   POET(anag)
24 VAUGHAN
26 RO<SS/IN>I
27 E/MU
28 UR/G/ENCY(clopaedia)
29 MARVELL
30 HER/RICK
31 HER/BERT

DOWN

1 LOVE/LACE
2 SUCKLING
3 IN/T<RIG>UES
4 NO/S<EG>AY
5 MAFIOSO (anag)
6 DONNE (done)
7 MIL/TON
8 DRYDEN
15 PYE (pie)
16 TREA(d)/SURER
17 I/N<DIG>ENE
18 CHAIN/LET(ter)
20 VA<N EY>C/K
21 NKRUMAH (hidden)
22 A/V/OUCH
23 MUGGER
25 HIND/I

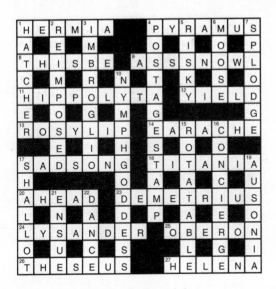

Theme: Couples in *A Midsummer Night's Dream*.

ACROSS

1   HER/MIA(rev)
4   (pa)PYR<AM>US
8   THIS/BE (Flute)
9   AS/S'<S NOW>L (III 2 17)
11 HIP/POLYTA(anag)
12 YIELD
13 ROS<Y L(eh)>IP (*Sonnet 116*)
14 E/ARACH(n)E
17 SAD SONG (anag)
18 TITANIA (pl of Titanium)
20 A/HEAD
23 DE<METRI>US
24 LY<SAND>ER
25 OBE/RON
26 THE/S(outh)E(ast)/US
27 HELENA (state capital)

DOWN

1   (t)HATCHER
2   REIMPOSED (anag)
3   I'M/BRO/GLI(s)/O
4   PO<STAGE 'S/TA>MP
5   RI/SKY
6   MOO/S/E
7   SP/LODGE
10 NYMPH GODDESS (III.2.137)
15 ROT/A/TABLE
16 CONCIERGE (anag)
17 SH<ALL>OT
19 AU/SONIA
21 (m)EN/SUE
22 DANCE (hidden)

159

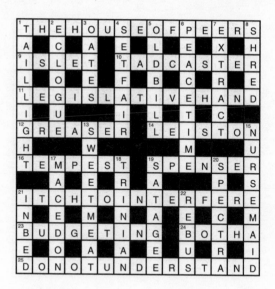

ACROSS

1,11,21,25 (And while) THE HOUSE OF
PEERS (anag) (cf song 'Bow,
bow, etc') *WIT/H H/OLD/S ITS*
LEG/IS/L<AT/IV/E H>AND,
*AN<D> NO/BLE ST/ATE'S/
MEN D/O N/OT* IT/CH
<TO> IN/TERFERE (anag) *IN
MATTERS WHICH THEY (anag)*
DO NOT/ UNDER/STAND,
(as bright will shine Great Britain's
rays) (Gilbert, *Iolanthe* Act 2, song
of Lord Mountararat, verse 3).

9 IS/LET
10 TAD/CASTER
12 GRE<AS>ER
14 L<E>ISTON
16 TEMPEST
19 SPENS/ER
23 BUDGE/TIN/G
24 BOTH/A

DOWN

1 TAIL/ LIGHT
2 E/C<LOG>UE
3 OATES (oats)
4 SET/ FAIR
5 OLD BILL
6 PEA/CETIME(anag)
7 EX/TRACT
8 SH<R>ED
13 SWEET/MEAT
15 NURSEMAID (anag)
17 MACE/DON
18 TRINI(dad/i)AN
19 SAT A GEE (*Pirates of Penzance*)
20 SPEC/TRA (all rev)
21 IN BED
22 REBUS

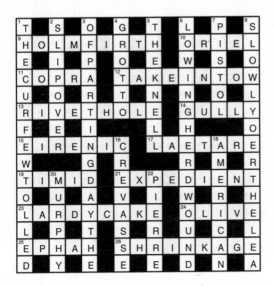

ACROSS

9 HOLM/FIRTH
10 ORIEL
11 COP/RA
12 TAKE IN TOW (anag)
13 RI<VET/ HO>LE
14 GULL/Y
15 EIRE/NIC
17 LAET/ARE (all rev)
19 TIM/ID
21 EX/PE<DIE>NT
23 LARDY-CAKE (anag)
24 O/LIVE
25 EPHAH (hidden)
26 SHRINK/AGE

DOWN

1,5,3,6,8 THE CUR/FEW/ TOLLED/
THE K/NELL/ OF/
PARTING/ DAY/ TH<E/
LOW>ING/ HE(a)RD/
WOUND S/LOWLY/ O'ER
THE LEA(anag)
2 SLIP/OVER
3 See 1
4 GROTTO
5 See 1
6 See 1
7 PISTOL
8 See 1
16 C<REV/ASS>E
18 A/MERI/CAN
20 MURPHY
22 P<I/ERR>E (gym)

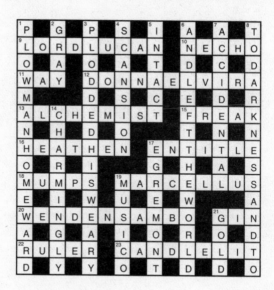

The spelling PLOWMAN is not, I confess, Gray's, but that of Piers and the King James Bible: Shakespeare uses both spellings.

ACROSS

9 LORD LUCAN (anag)
10 N/ECHO
11 See 1
12 DONNA ELVIRA (anag)
13 AL/CHE/MIST
15 F<R>E/A/K
16 HEAT/HEN
17 ENT/I/TLE
18 MUM/P'S
19 MAR<CELL/U>S
20 WEN/DEN/S AMBO
21 GIN
22 RULER
23 CAN<DLE-L>/IT

DOWN

1,3,11,6,8,2 PLOWMAN/
HO<MEW>ARD/
P/L/ODD/ED/
H/I/S WEAR/(m)Y WAY/
AND/ LEFT THE WORLD/
TO D/ARK/NESS/
AND <TO /G/RA>Y
2 See 1
3 See 1
4 SCAN/SION
5 (p)INTA/C(a)T
6 See 1
7 ACCIDENTAL
8 See 1
14 CHAR<MING/L>Y
17 EG<RE>MONT
19 MUSICO (anag) (Heavy Dragoon song)
21 GOLD

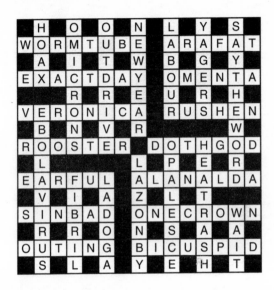

Perimeter: THEY ALSO SERVE WHO ONLY STAND AND [WAIT] (Milton, *Sonnet on his Blindness*).

1 A/LAN A/LDA
2 A/RA/FAT
3 BI/CU<S>PID
4,7,11 DOT/H <GO/D [EXACT DAY] LAB(rev)>OUR
5 EARFUL (anag)
6 EBOLA VIRUS (anag)
7 See 4
8 FIB/R<I>L
9 HE/A/T RASH
10 HO/AX
11 See 4
12 L<A/DOG>A
13 LAZ<ON/B>Y
14 NE<W YE>AR

15 OMENTA (hidden)
16 (c)OMIC/(se)RONS(rev)
17 O<NE CRO(polis)>WN
18 O/PALES/CE
19 OUTDRIVE (anag)
20 OUTING
21 RO<O>STER
22 RUSH(d)EN
23 SAY THE WORD (anag)
24 SIN/BAD
25 VERONICA (anag)
26 W<A>IT
27 WORM TUBE (anag)
28 YAGERS (anag)

PARIS IS (merely) AN ABBREVIATION OF PARADISE.

1 BERK(shire)/HAMSTE(r)/D
2 BUFFS
3 CHER<NOB>YL
4 DI<SP/ROPE>RTY
5 DO/MINATOR(y)
6 DU<MBE>ST
7 EIGHTEEN (anag)
8 FOLD IN TWO (anag)
9 FRO<W>ST
10 GAM(rev)/BIAN(co)
11 H/ARD NUT (rev)
12 HO<I>ST
13 IN/STANCE
14 MI<TT>EN
15 MO/IRA
16 OH D(ode)/EAR

17 RAN UP
18 R/E/LEAR/N
19 RE/TREATED
20 RUN
21 SANDRA (hidden)
22 SPEED/STER
23 STAITHE (anag)
24 ST NEOTS (anag)
25 'TAIN'T
26 T/ALLY
27 TEAR/SHEET
28 THOU/SAND
29 ULT (hidden)
30 (t)UNIC/OR/N
31 VERT/ICES
32 WINE BAR (anag)

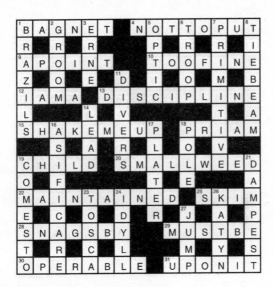

The crossword grid reads:

B	A	G	N	E	T		N	O	T	T	O	P	U	T
R		R		R			P		R		R		I	
A	P	O	I	N	T		T	O	O	F	I	N	E	
Z		O		E		D	I		O		M		B	
I	A	M	A		D	I	S	C	I	P	L	I	N	E
L			L		V					T		A		
S	H	A	K	E	M	E	U	P		P	R	I	A	M
	S		A		R		L		O		V			
C	H	I	L	D		S	M	A	L	L	W	E	E	D
O		F				T		E					A	
M	A	I	N	T	A	I	N	E	D		S	K	I	M
E		C		O		D		R		J		A		P
S	N	A	G	S	B	Y		M	U	S	T	B	E	
T		R		L						M		Y		S
O	P	E	R	A	B	L	E		U	P	O	N	I	T

Theme: Characters from *Bleak House* with their repeated utterances.

ACROSS

1	BAG/NET
4,10,9,31	NOT TO PUT TOO FINE A POINT UPON IT
12,19	I/A/M A CH/I'LD
13,29,22	DISCIPLINE MUST BE MAINTAINED (anag)
15	S<HAKE/ ME U>P
18	PR/IAM
19	See 12
20	SMALL/WEED
22	See 13
25,18dn	SKIM/POLE
28	SNAGS/BY
29	See 13
30	OPERABLE
31	See 4

DOWN

1	B/RA<Z>ILS
2	GROOM
3	ERNE(st)
5	OPT/I/C
6	T/ROOP (rev)
7	P<RIM>IT/I'VE
8	TIE/ BEAM
11	DIVERS
14	See 27
16	AS IF I CARE (anag)
17	PLATER
18	See 25
19	COMES T(ibles)/O
21	DAM/PEST
23	TOSCA (anag)
24	IDYLL (anag)
26	K/A/TYN(e)
27,14	JUM(bos)/P LEAD

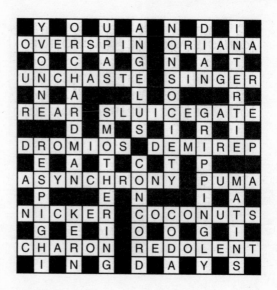

YOU AND I ARE PAST OUR DANCING DAYS (*Romeo and Juliet* I.5.35)
(the title is from line 32).

1 ANG<EL>US
2 A/SYN/C<H>RONY*
3 CHAR/ON
4 CO/CO/NUTS
5 COD/A
6 CON/CORD
7 DE<MIR>EP
8 (come)DIAN
9 (c)D-ROM/I/OS
10 G/RIPPING/LY
11 INTER/TIE
12 KERN
13 MATINS (anag)
14 NICKER
15 NON-SOCIETY

16 ORC/HARD MAN
17 (vict)ORIANA
18 OVER/SPIN
19 PU/MA (rev)
20 R/EAR
21 RE<DOLE>NT
22 RESPIGHI (hidden)
23 SINGER
24 SLU<ICE>G/ATE
25 S/MOTHERING
26 (l)UNCH/AS/TE(a)
27 U/PAS
28 Y<V>ONNE

*Dr Syn books by Russell Thorndike

Perimeter: THE <GL>ORIES/ O/F OUR /BL<OOD AND (anag)> STATE (anag) (*Death the Leveller* by James Shirley).

1 ANDREA (hidden)
2 B/ONE
3 CEP/HALO/POD
4 C<HEAP/ENIN(rev)>G
5 (man)DELA/NO (FDR)
6 D/I/S/P/I/R/I/T
7 (t)EM<ERY PA(anag)>PER
8 F<LANDER>S
9 GRADIENT (anag)
10 IN<SPA>N
11 LESS/EPS
12 (e)LUR/GAN (rev)
13 MON/DEO
14 OAK LEATHER (anag)

15 ODER/ZO(rev)
16 ONCE
17 ONCE MORE
18 R<EG>AIN
19 REIN/DEER
20 RE/PEAL
21 RIAH (rev)
22 SH<AD>OWS
23 SHIRLEY
24 SORT (hidden)
25 TORT/ILL/A
26 UNCLE/N/CH
27 UPSTAGE (anag)
28 WARP/LANE

Theme: Poets Laureate (whose 'numbers' won the 'laurel').

ACROSS

1 COMEDOWN (O maid from yonder mountain height)
5 GLO(w)/BED (Ode to Melancholy)
9 BATS/FORD
10 AUSTIN
11 EX<ORC>IST
12 BE<HE>AD
14 ROYAL TRAIN
18 STAG/NATION
22 HU(GH)ES
23 MO<NUMEN>T
24 WART/ON
25 SHAD/WELL
26 DRY/DEN
27 TENNYS/ON

DOWN

1 CIBBER (anag, I for A)
2 MOTION
3 DEF(rev)/ACE
4 WORDS/WORTH
6 L/AUREATE
7 BE/TJE/MAN
8 DING-DONG
13 M<AC>ONOCHIE (monarchy)
15 ES<CHEW>ED
16 BADGE/RLY
17 ANT/ELOPE
19 EUS/DEN (all rev)
20 RECESS
21 ST<OL>EN

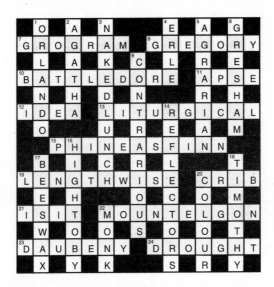

Theme: Fellow MPs of Phineas Finn (Trollope).

ACROSS

7 GROG/RAM
8 G/RE/GORY
10 B/ATTLE<DOR(rev)>E
11 AP<S>E
12 I/DEA(d)
13 LIT//(s)URGICAL
15 PH/INEAS F(anag)/INN
19 LENGTHWISE (anag)
20 CRIB
21 I S/IT (Christopher Robin)
22 MO<UN>T EL/GON(e)
23 DA<U/BEN>Y
24 DR/OUGHT

DOWN

1 ORLANDO
2 A/GAT/HA(s)
3 NAKED LUNCH
4 (Mand)ERLE(y)
5 AGRA/RIAN
6 GRESHAM
9 CONTRARIOUS (anag)
14 RE<FLE(rev)>CTORS
16 HIGH T/O/BY
17 BEES/WAX
18 TI/MOTH/Y
20 COL/OUR
22 MON/K

See *The Winter's Tale* III.2.133.

ACROSS

1 S/HARP (#)
4 CO<HES/IB>LE
9 BA<RILL>A
10 RE/A/WAKE
11 ESSE/X
12 TR<I/TEN>ESS
13 T<YRAN(rev)>T
15 ONCE SEEN (anag) (never forgotten)
18 CRY/OST/A/T
19 OPUSES (anag)
22 MUL(e)/TI<P>ARA
24,1dn A TRUE SUBJECT
26 LE(e)/ON/TE(e)S
27 JE/A/LOU(i)S
28 ORDER/ A/RMS
29 ENTER(ic) (computing)

DOWN

1 See 24
2 ARRAS (Polonius)
3 POLIXENES
4 CHASTE (chased)
5 HERMI(t)/ONE
6 STALE (*Much Ado About Nothing* IV.1.64)
7 B<LAME>LESS
8 (p)E<ME>RSON
14 ROYAL ROAD (anag)
16 ES<PLAN/AD>E
17 MA/C<ASS>AR
18 C<A/MILL>O
20 S/PENS/ER
21 HADJIS (jihads)
23 INTER
25 RO<OS>T

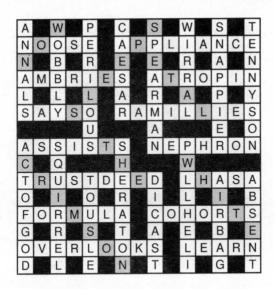

NOW SLEEPS THE CRIMSON PETAL, NOW THE WHITE (anag).

1 AB/SENT
2 AC/T O<F/ GO>D
3 AIRBAG
4 AM/BRIES
5 ANNA/L/S
6 APPL<I/ANC>E
7 ASSI<ST>S(i)
8 A<TROPI(c)>N
9 CAESAR (seizer)
10 CO<H/OR>TS
11 DI(e)/CAST
12 FORMULA
13 LEAR/N
14 L/HAS/A
15 NEP(rev)/HR/ON

16 NOOS(rev)/E
17 OVER/LOOKS
18 PERILOUS (anag)
19 PWLLHELI (anag)
20 RA<MILLIE>S
21 SAY-S/O
22 SHE/RAT/ON
23 SNAP/PIER
24 SPE<ARM>AN
25 S/QUI<RRE(rev)>L(l)
26 TENNYSON (venison)
27 TOUSLE (anag)
28 TRUST/ DEED
29 WIRRAL
30 WOBBLY

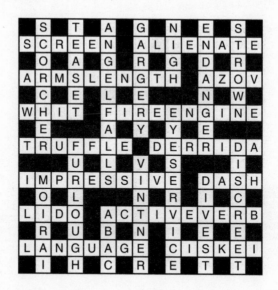

Perimeter: ST AGNES EVE, AH BITTER CHILL IT WAS (Keats).

1 ABAC(i)
2 ACT/IV/E VER/B
3 A/LIEN/A/TE(n)
4 ANGEL FALLS
5 ARMS LENGTH
6 A/ZO/V (rev)
7 CISKEI (hidden)
8 DASH
9 D<ERR>ID/A
10 DISC/REET
11 DIVES/T
12 END/ANGER
13 E<YE-S>E'R/VICE
14 F<I/RE ENG(anag)>INE

15 FUR/LOUGH
16 GAR(a)GE/RY
17 I'M/PRESS/I'VE
18 LANG/U/AGE
19 LID/O
20 MOIRA/I
21 NIGH(t)
22 SCOR<CH>ER
23 SCREEN
24 S<TROW>N
25 TEA SET (anag)
26 T/RUFFLE
27 VINT<N>ER
28 WHIT

Perimeter: [Indeed, indeed, repentance oft before] I SWORE, BUT WAS I SOBER WHEN I SWORE? (anag) [and then and then came spring] (*Omar* I.70 or II.102).

1 ANT/ENNAE (any)
2 BE/AN/POLE
3 BEAU/LIE/U
4 CLAVIS (Clovis)
5 EL/LIP/TICAL (tickle)
6 E<MP>IRE
7 (swin)G/LOW
8 HALL/ELU(i)JAH
9 HU<MO/URLE>SS
10 IMP/UGN(anag)
11 INDULGENCE (anag)
12 MIN/DER
13 MINI (hidden)
14 MO/AB

15 NAV<(a)ARON>E
16 OB/LO/NG
17 ON <THE> NIGHT (anag)
18 PROFI<CIEN>T
19 RA(b)BI
20 RUIN (Curse upon Edward)
21 SAN/ZIO
22 SIGN
23 STY/E
24 T<RACH(anag)>EA
25 TROW(bridge, Wilts)
26 TURBULENCE (anag)
27 WAL(rev)/L MAP(anag)
28 WEE/PIN/G ASH

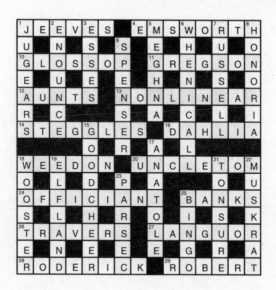

Title: P G Wodehouse (seventeen solutions refer to his characters).

ACROSS

1 JE/EVE'S
4 EMSWORTH (anag)
10 G<LOSS>O/P
11 See 9
12 AUNTS
13 N/ON-LI/NEAR
14 ST/EGG/LES
16 DAHLIA
18 WEE/DON
20 UNCLE/ TOM
24 OFF/I/C<I>ANT
25 BANKS
26 T/RAVERS
27 LANGU<O>R
28 RODE/RICK
29 ROBERT(a)

DOWN

1 JU/G-EARS
2 ENOUNCE (hidden)
3 ESSES
5 MEG<HN>A
6 W<HEN/ I C>ALL
7 RUSSELL (rustle)
8 HO/NO/RIA
9,11 SPENS/ER G/REGS/ON (Aunt
   Agatha)
15 GO/OD <CHE>ER
17 AN/A<TO>LE
18 WOOSTER (anag)
19 EL<FLAN>D (Tennyson, Princess)
21 TON/SURE
22 MUS<K-RA>T
23 PARSE/C
25 BIN/GO

Perimeter: THE CAPTAINS AND THE KINGS DEPART (Kipling, *Recessional*, v2).

1 A/BASHED
2 A/GOUT/I
3 (dism)ANTLERS
4 A/T<RAM>ENT
5 BROILERS
6 C<O>AT
7 DART/LE
8 DIES (latin)
9 DR/ON/GO
10 E/LATER/IN
11 ESCUDO (anag)
12 HE/CUB/A
13 LONG /LAST
14 LUTHERAN (anag)

15 PAR/TY P<IE/C>E
16 PER/NOD
17 POLO
18 POW/(ei)DER DOWN
19 PUN/K
20 RA<ZOR-[ST]RO>P
21 SECRET/A
22 SHEP<PER>TON
23 SHOUTING (anag)
24 TEASPOON
25 TO/READ/OR
26 TUM/ULT
27 WHO/O/SH
28 Z/WING/L/I

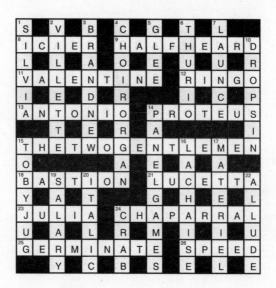

Theme: *The Two Gentlemen of Verona*. They loved (for a time) the same lady; the dog is at 24.

ACROSS

8 ICI/ER
9 HALF HEARD (anag) (Lepanto)
11 V<A/LENT>INE
12 RING/O
13 ANT/ONIO(n)
14 PROTEUS (anag)
15 THE TWO GENTLEMEN (anag)
18 B<ASTI>ON
21 LU/CETTA (lieu setter)
23 JULIA(n)
24 CHAP/AR<R>AL
25 G<ERMIN(e)>ATE
26 SPEED

DOWN

1 SILVIA
2 VILLETTE
3 BRAN/D-NEW(rev)
4 CHOIR ORGAN (anag)
5 GLEE
6 THUR/IO
7 LAUNCE
10 DROP/S IN
14 PANEL GAMES (anag)
15 TOBY/-JUGS
16 (père) LA/CHAISE
17 MAT/ERIE/L
19 SA<LAR>Y
20 ITALIC
22 ALL/UDE (anag)
24 CRAB

T	H	E	P	R	O	P		
N	I	C	E		L	A	R	G	E	S	C	A	L	E

Perimeter: (Know then thyself: presume not God to scan) THE
P<R>**OPE**R STUDY OF MANKIND IS MAN.

1 AREZZO	15 NANCY/ AS/TOR
2 AU/SPICES	16 NICE
3 COPYIST (anag)	17 (j)OCULAR
4 D<ERR>IS	18 PLAITERS (platters)
5 ÉC/LAIR	19 PRES(s)/U/ME
6 ELECT/RON/IC	20 PRO <RAT>A
7 HELP/MEET	21 REDE (hidden)
8 IRIS/H CAR	22 REL/I/SHED
9 LARGE-SCALE	23 SCAN
10 LA<Z>Y	24 (he)S/MET/AN/A(ctor)
11 MA/U/ MA/U	25 STORM AL(anag)/ARM
12 METEOR (anag)	26 S/TRUCK
13 MI/SERIES	27 TIT/(y)ULE
14 MORDECA(anag)/I	28 YOURSELF (anag)

See 'Where the remote Bermudas ride' (poem by Marvell).

ACROSS

8 EQUIN(e)/OX
9 BERMUDA
10 See 14
11 NUR(rev)/SERIES
13 See 14
14,22,10,3,13 HE HANGS IN SHADES/
    THE ORANGE BRIGHT/
    LIKE GOLDEN LAMPS
    (carol is 'Like silver lamps in
    a distant shrine the stars are
    sparkling bright')/ IN <A
    GREE>N/ NIGH/T
18 S<TAR>S
20 RI<SING> SUN
22 See 14
24 FAL/ANGE
25 DISTANT

DOWN

1 KELLY/N/CH (*Persuasion*)
2 PUCK/ER
3 See 14
4 AXE/L
5 DRAL/ON (rev)
6 RUM/MAGE/D
7 B<ASS>ET
9 B<LESS>INGS (Barbara Pym
   novel)
12 INSURANCE (anag)
15 HE<AVE>NLY
16 HUN/TRESS
17 SAN<CT>ITY
18 SET OFF
19 SH<R>INE
21 SIGNAL
23 EDDY

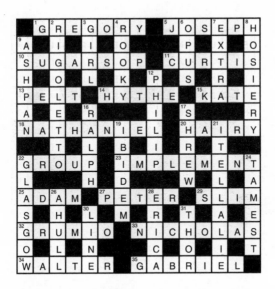

Solutions to asterisked clues are servants of Petruchio (*The Taming of the Shrew* IV.1.128).

ACROSS

1 G<REG>ORY
5 JOS<EP>H
10 SUGARSO(a)P
11 CUR/TIS
13 PELT
14 H/Y/THE
15 KATE
18 NATHANIE(anag)/L
20 HAIRY
22 GRO(w)/UP
23 IMPLEMENT
25 ADAM
27 PETER
29,30 SLIMLINE (anag)
32 G/RUM/IO
33 NICHOLAS (S Claus: nick)
34,35 WALTER: GABRIEL

DOWN

2 RIGOLETTO (anag)
3 GI/R/L
4 ROOKY (*Macbeth* III.2.51)
6 O/PUS
7 EXTRA (hidden)
8 (wit)H<OSIER>Y
9 ASH-/PAN
12 PHILIP (Bastard, Fr king)(fillip)
16 R/ALPH
17 SH<R>EW
19 I<BIDE>'M
21 I T/EL(u)L A LIE
22 G/LAS(s)/GO/W(est)
24 T<A/M>EST
26 A/HULL
28 ERICA (anag)
30 See 29
31 THOR (hidden)

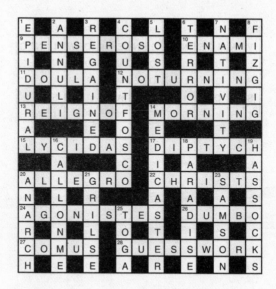

Title quotation from Wordsworth's 'Scorn not the sonnet'.

ACROSS

9 PEN/S<EROS>O
10 E/N`A/M'I (rev)
11 DOULA (anag)
12 NO TURNING
13,6 REIGN (rain)/ OF T/ERROR
14 of 22 7 MORNING of CHRIST'S NATIVITY (anag)
15 LYCIDAS (anag – Lady C is)
17 DIP/TYCH(o)
20 ALL/EG/RO
22 See 14
24 See 23
26 DUMB/O
27 CO(mpany)/MUS(rev)
28 GU<ESSWO(anag)>RK(rev)

DOWN

1 E/P<IDUR>AL
2 ANNUL/I
3 R<EG>AINED
4 CO<UNT FOS(anag)>CO
5 LO/ST (sonnet on his deceased wife)
6 See 13
7 See 14ac
8 FI<Z/GI>G
14 MEDIC/ASTER
16 CALL ON ME (anag)
18 PARAD<IS>E
19 HAS/SOCKS
20 AN/ARCH
21 GRI<L>SE
23,24 S<AM/SO[N AG]ON>IST/E/S
25 TO/GA

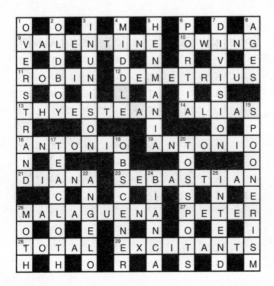

Theme: Different Shakespeare characters with the same name clued by their utterances.

ACROSS

9 VALENTINE (*Two Gentlemen of Verona* V.4.170; *Twelfth Night* I.1.30)
10 O/WING
11 ROBIN (*A Midsummer Night's Dream* II.1.43; *Merry Wives of Windsor* III.3.24)
12 DEMETRIUS (*Titus Andronicus* II.1.82; *A Midsummer Night's Dream* III.2.143)
13 THY/ESTE/A/N
14 A/LIAS
16 ANTONIO (*The Tempest* II.1.291; *Merchant of Venice* IV.1.281)
19 ANTONIO (*Twelfth Night* I.1.48; *Much Ado About Nothing* IV.1.91)
21 DIANA (*Pericles* V.1.241; *All's Well That Ends Well* IV.2.54)
23 SEBASTIAN (*The Tempest* II.1.263; *Twelfth Night* V.1.236)
26 MA/LAGU<E>NA
27 PETER (*Measure for Measure* V.1.139; *Romeo and Juliet* IV.5.146)
28 TOTAL (anag)
29 EX<CI>TANT'S

DOWN

1 O/VERST/R/AND
2 OLD BOY
3 I/N UN/I/SON
4,8 MID<DLE A>GES
5 HEN/MAN/I/A
6 PORTIA (*Julius Caesar* II.1.274; *Merchant of Venice* IV.1.252)
7 DI/VISION
8 See 4
15 SPOONERISM (anag)
17 TEA C/LOTH
18 OB<SCENE>R
20 TOS(rev)/SPOTS
22 ANGELO (*The Comedy of Errors* V.1.380; *Measure for Measure* II.1.144)
24 BIANCA (*Othello* V.1.77; *The Taming of the Shrew* V.2.46)
25 IN/TEND
26 MOTH (*Love's Labours Lost* V.1.39; *A Midsummer Night's Dream* III.1.170, 184)

Title quotation from Tennyson, 'Locksley Hall': 'In the spring a livelier iris...'
Theme: Iris Murdoch novels.

ACROSS

1,7 UNOFFICIAL ROSE
9 FLIGHT
10,13 A S/EVER/ED/ HEAD
11 CAPRI/AT/I
12 P/LENT/Y
13 See 10
15 SAN(d) MARTIN
17 CONSTRUCT (anag)
20 See 5
21 BAR<TO>K
23 ICE CREAM (I scream)
25 STACCATO (anag)
26 THE SE/A (the sea)
27 IRIS
28 SANDCASTLE

DOWN

2 NULL/A (a/void)
3 FIGURED
4 IN/ TRANSIT
5,20ac ITALIAN GIRL (anag)
6 LIE U/P
7 RE-EL/ECT
8 S/WEE/TEN/ER
14 ENCHANTER (hidden)
16 AU<THE>NT/I/C
18 NOT/ICES
19 UNI/CORN
20 G/ARDENS
22 KEATS (anag)
24 A (the) BELL

CD in title = Charles Dickens.

A AUNT (haunt)
B BRASS
C COPPER/FIELD
D DE/SERVING
E E/IDER
F FREE-TRADERS (anag)
G GRADGRIND (grid grand)
H HAWKBELLS (anag)
I I/NUIT (Fr)
J JEMMY
K K/ENG/E
L L/UXU(o)RIOUS
M M/ANTALINI (anag)

N NISAN (nice Anne)
O OVER/LOO/KING
P PINCH
Q QUI<L>P
R RIAH (hair)
S SUMMER/SON
T T<'ULKING>HORN
U (g)UN/DO(g)
V VENUS
W W<HIT>E
X XI/P<HI/IDA>E
Y Y(o)UMA (3.10 to …)
Z ZA<BRISK>I(r)E (Z point)